The Desire To Love Myself

expanded

robyn michelle

i

Library of Congress Control Number: 2025905674
Published in Carolina Beach, NC
Publication Cataloging-in-Publication Data
Paperback ISBN: 979-8-9920625-2-6
eBook ISBN: 979-8-9920625-1-9
Printed in the United States of America

ii

DEDICATION

This book is dedicated to those who laugh with me until we're crying and cry with me until we're laughing.

CONTENTS

Introduction

Have you ever truly allowed yourself to dream about the future you want? Not just a passing thought, but a deep, immersive vision of the life you desire? Close your eyes for a moment, take a deep breath, and picture yourself five years from now—ten years from now. Where are you? What are you doing? Who is with you? Imagine the details vividly. Do you hear the laughter of loved ones in your dream home? Do you feel the excitement of stepping onto a plane for that long-awaited adventure? Can you smell the fresh pages of a book you've always wanted to write or the aroma of success in a business you built from the ground up? Let your imagination embrace every moment, every sound, every feeling of joy and fulfillment.

Now, hold onto that vision. How does it make you feel? Empowered? Capable? Inspired? Good—because that dream is not out of reach. It's not some distant fantasy; it's a future waiting for you to claim it.

The secret is this: You can live the life you dream of. No dream is too big, and no goal is too far away. Dreams are part of what makes you unique; they are designed for you and by you. No matter where you are right now, you have the power to begin making changes. One step at a time, one decision at a time, you can move toward that vision and make it your reality.

Of course, making dreams come true doesn't happen overnight. It takes dedication, persistence, and resilience. But every journey starts with a single step. The key is to focus your energy and take action, one step at a time.

There are countless examples of people who refused to let obstacles stand in their way. One of the most well-known is J.K. Rowling, who overcame poverty, rejection, and personal hardship before becoming one of the most successful authors of all time. She left an abusive marriage, struggled as a single mother, and faced multiple rejections before finally getting her first book published. But she didn't give up. She held onto her dream, took consistent action, and changed the course of her life.

But you don't have to be the creator of a beloved famous wizard to create your own success story. You, too, can be someone who inspires others with your journey—someone who overcame doubt, fear, and adversity to achieve something incredible. Your future success story starts now, and one day, you'll look back and realize that every step, every setback, and every victory shaped the person you were meant to become.

Maybe you're feeling stuck. Maybe you're unsure where to begin. No matter your current circumstances, you have the power to stop, reassess, and change direction. If you feel lost or discouraged, know this: The path to your dreams is still open. You are not too late, not too far behind, and you are capable.

I am here to remind you that you are not alone. We all face struggles, doubts, and setbacks. Together, we can lift each other up, push forward, and make meaningful progress. There is strength in numbers, and when we support one another, we accomplish more than we ever could alone.

This is the beginning of a journey—one where we navigate life's toughest challenges, push past fears, and move toward the future we deserve. Are you ready to take that first step?

Take a deep breath, write down three small actions you can take this week to move closer to your dream, and let's begin.

Affirmation: I am capable, worthy, and ready to step into the life I envision. Every step I take brings me closer to my dreams, and I trust the journey ahead.

Journal Prompt: What does your dream life look like in vivid detail? Describe a day in your ideal future, from the moment you wake up to the moment you go to sleep. How do you feel? What steps can you take today to bring that vision closer to reality?

Stranded or Set Free

When watching a movie like *Cast Away* or a television series such as *Naked and Afraid*, I often find myself wondering, *Could I survive if I were stranded on a desert island?* Survival-type shows always get my problem-solving brain turning. Maybe you've had similar thoughts. *What would I do in their place? How would I create shelter? What would I eat to survive?* If it rained, would I know how to keep myself warm and dry?

To say I dislike being wet and cold is an understatement. I'm not a Girl Scout, and I have no survival skills or wilderness training of any kind. I'd like to believe I could fashion some sort of shelter, but if we're placing bets on my survival, don't bother— I'd likely fall ill from sun poisoning, and call it quits. If I ever find myself shipwrecked on some remote island, don't count on my resilience—just send help!

Yet, in a way, I have been stranded before. Not on a physical island, but in a place of uncertainty, transition, and reinvention. That's where my real survival story begins.

Far from a deserted beach, I now find myself in a little Coastal Carolina town, hundreds of miles from everyone and everything I once knew. A fresh start. A blank slate. For the first time in forty-five years, I found myself truly on my own. I moved knowing little more than the fact that the weather was perfect for a summer-lover like me and that the ocean was close enough to hear the waves when the wind was just right.

It wasn't just a move—it was a *choice*. A declaration that my life wasn't going to pass me by while I sat idly, waiting for "one day" to arrive.

The Danger of "One Day"

So often we say to ourselves, *One day I'm going to...* But then one day turns into another, and another, and another, until it simply never comes. Life gets in the way. Excuses pile up. We tell ourselves we'll get to it later, when things are more stable, when the timing is right, when we feel ready.

But readiness is a mirage. There will never be a perfect time to take a leap of faith. If we wait for that elusive moment when all the stars align, we'll wake up years from now wondering why we never took the chance.

I refused to let that happen. Not this time.

Much like the contestants on survival shows, I had to learn how to navigate my own new wilderness. It wasn't about spearing fish or foraging for edible plants, it was about establishing a foundation in unfamiliar territory.

The Courage to Choose Change

Why such a drastic change halfway through your forties? Why embark on such a journey *alone?*

Because sometimes life reaches a breaking point, a moment when staying the same becomes more uncomfortable than the fear of change. Sometimes, you realize you've been *surviving* for so long that you've forgotten what it means to truly *live.*

And so, I jumped.

This wasn't a decision made overnight, nor was it one driven by recklessness. It was a choice to step into something new, something that had the potential to change everything. And despite the uncertainty, I knew in my bones it was the right decision.

It's Never Too Late

Pursuing your dreams doesn't require a tragic backstory or a dramatic life event. Yes, for some, myself included, pain and hardship have served as catalysts for transformation. But change doesn't have to come from struggle.

It can come simply from a desire to chase the things that set your soul on fire.

Too often, we let distractions, setbacks, and the doubts of others keep us from moving forward. The road to our dreams is rarely smooth, it's full of obstacles, self-doubt, and moments that test our resolve. But none of those things have the power to stop you unless you let them.

As I open up about my journey, I hope it serves as encouragement that you, too, have the power to create the life you want. I hope you'll be reminded that *it's never too late* to dream a new dream, to rewrite your story, and to take the first step toward a future that excites you.

This is your *one* life.

Make sure you're living it.

Affirmation: I am brave enough to follow my dreams, trusting that every step I take brings me closer to my true purpose. I embrace the unknown with courage, knowing that I am capable of achieving everything I desire.

Journal Prompt: Think about a moment in your life when you faced uncertainty or change. How did you respond to it? What fears or doubts did you need to overcome to move forward? If you could make one bold

Grow Through What You Go Through

Life has a way of throwing obstacles in our path when we least expect them. Sometimes, they're like hidden roots beneath our feet, small, unexpected, and easy to recover from. Other times, they're like massive, immovable boulders that crash into our lives, leaving us breathless and broken. We trip, we fall, and sometimes we wonder if we'll ever get up again. We'd be hard-pressed to find someone who can honestly say they've never faced a challenge or heartache that set them back or knocked them off course. But what if, instead of seeing these obstacles as barriers, we remind ourselves that they are part of the path itself, twists in the journey that lead us somewhere new, somewhere better?

Being knocked down provides the opportunity to get back up stronger than before. While being punched in the gut sucks a big one, it can show you how incredibly tough you are. Carry the world on your shoulders, because then you will find out just how strong you are. Let the haters and gossipers talk because you'll get to feel the satisfaction that comes when they're silenced.

Embrace every challenge, letting your passion be set on fire through a heart of resilience.

We admire the strongest people not because they have never fallen, but because they have risen despite every setback. Think of anyone who has ever achieved greatness, their journeys are never smooth. Whether it's the athlete who missed the winning shot, the entrepreneur who faced bankruptcy before success, or the single parent struggling to rebuild a life, resilience is what makes the difference. When life hits hard, it's okay to feel the pain, but don't let it define you. Let it shape you into something stronger

You do not have to be okay with what you're going through, of course, but use it. Use what impacted you to empower you—to be a driving force propelling you toward what is next, toward your true calling. As you maneuver through life's obstacles, ask yourself, "What can I learn? How can I grow? How can I serve the needs of others, change my surroundings, and help those around me?" As you continue moving forward and learn the answers to those questions, ask yourself, "What can I change, and what steps do I need to take so I can be where I want to be, where I am meant to be?"

Robert Frost said, "The best way out is always through," and honestly, it's the only way. As much as we want to, there is no way to avoid a situation before you and the emotions entangled with it. You must experience and endure it as best as you can while moving steadily through it. Choosing not to do so only prolongs the inevitable.

Frost's famous words were sent to me amid the deepest, lowest, most heart breaking time of my life. I will never forget them; they will forever be etched to the core of my being. I will always remember the feeling that came over me as I read them, and how deeply my heart sank. As true as they are, they were the last words I wanted to hear, as at that very moment I was struck with the realization of how difficult the road ahead would truly be. All I wanted to do was avoid what was before me, and either go back in time or skip to the good part. I had just discovered my husband was having an affair. We'd only been married for five years, but I was madly in love with him and completely blindsided by this discovery.

A few weeks prior he said he was unhappy, but I thought we could work on our marriage, make some positive changes for the both of us and fix what seemed to be breaking down. Little did I know I was engaging in what would inevitably become a losing battle. His mind and his heart had already been given to another. Sadly, this was my second marriage, the one that was supposed to be blessed, supposed to work out, the one I thought I deserved after surviving a sixteen-year marriage plagued by verbal and mental abuse. In my first marriage, we stayed together far too long, but did it for the kids, and because "that's what good Christians do." When it escalated to him threatening to kill me in front of our son, I finally found the strength to walk away. Did I think he would follow through with the threat? No. But that was the moment I decided our children deserved a better example of a loving relationship and I deserved peace.

It took many months for me to move forward after each marriage. I didn't want to move through it; I barely wanted to move at all. I refused to feel anything after being knocked down, and I rejected any concept of finding a blessing in the trauma. My life was shattered, and I did not have any desire to pick up and piece together whatever shards remained. I felt paralyzed, betrayed, and lost. The pain was overwhelming, and hope felt out of reach. But healing isn't about one big breakthrough, it's about the small choices we make every day. Some days, it was simply getting out of bed and making coffee. Other days, it was reminding myself that I was worthy of love and happiness, even if I didn't fully believe it yet. Each tiny act of self-care, each moment of courage, built upon the last until I realized I wasn't just surviving, I was rebuilding.

Much like rainbows only come after it rains, I slowly began to see specks of color again. I started asking myself, "What do I want out of life? Who do I want to be? Where do I want to end up? What opportunities can I create for myself that I couldn't have or wouldn't have thought about before, and what steps do I need to take to make them happen?" As I began to move forward, I was determined to take control and stay in charge of my life, and you can too!

Maybe your heartbreak looks different than mine. Maybe it's a career that didn't pan out, a friendship that ended, or a dream that feels out of reach. Whatever it is, you are not alone. Pain and disappointment are part of life, but they are not the end of the story. You have the power to turn this moment into a catalyst for something greater. The question isn't whether you will get through it, it's how you will use it to fuel your next chapter.

No matter how broken you feel, you are not defeated. The hardest moments of our lives are often the ones that reveal our true strength. Take a deep breath, straighten your shoulders, and know this: You are capable of rebuilding. You are worthy of happiness. And you are stronger than you think.

Affirmation: I embrace life's obstacles as opportunities for growth, knowing that every challenge strengthens me and brings me closer to the person I am meant to become. I trust in my resilience and ability to navigate through any difficulty with grace and determination.

Journal Prompt: Reflect on a challenging experience you've gone through. At the time, it may have felt difficult or even unfair. Looking back, how did this experience contribute to your growth? What strengths or insights did you gain that you might not have discovered otherwise? How can you apply those lessons to your life moving forward?

Stepping Stones:

Turning Setbacks into Strength

Setbacks shall now be known as stepping stones. With a positive mindset, perseverance, and a plan, setbacks provide an opportunity to continually evaluate our goals and keep moving forward. They are not roadblocks meant to stop us but rather challenges designed to push us toward growth.

When you think about grief and the process of overcoming hardship, imagine embarking on a challenging hike. It's not a leisurely walk in the park where the entire path is paved, and you can see what's ahead. Instead, it's a rugged trail filled with peaks and valleys, unexpected obstacles, and moments where you have to stop and catch your breath. Sometimes, you'll feel steady, like you're making progress, but then you'll trip over an exposed root or stumble on loose gravel, bringing you back to an emotional place you thought you had left behind. Just when you think you're past the various stages of the grieving process, such as anger or sadness, a single moment—a song on the radio, a familiar scent, a casual mention of a name—can bring it all rushing back. It can hit you out of nowhere, leaving you wondering, "Where did this come from? I thought I had moved past this."

That's the thing about healing, it's not linear. There is no set timeline, no clear finish line. It's an unpredictable journey with highs and lows, setbacks and victories. But every step you take, even the difficult ones, moves you forward.

Not every day has to be, or will be, a ten-out-of-ten, dancing-in-the-kitchen kind of day. Some days will be a two-out-of-ten. That's okay. The tough days don't mean you're failing; they simply mean you're feeling. And feeling means you're alive, you're healing, and you're growing. Those low points make the good days all the more meaningful. Healing isn't about rushing through the hard parts; it's about allowing yourself the grace to move through them at your own pace.

When you feel like something has set you back, don't endure it alone. Always allow yourself to experience and feel your feelings. Give yourself the space to experience them fully because, remember, the only way out of a setback is through it. Momentarily embrace how you feel, then release it. But don't stay in a place of gloom and despair for too long. When you find yourself struggling, reach out, call a friend, send a text. There are people who truly want to be there for you, and they might be upset to learn that you needed help but didn't ask. Let them support you; lean on them.

Too often, we convince ourselves that asking for help is a burden, that people have their own problems, or that we should 'just deal with it.' Isolation only deepens the struggle. When we open up, we invite others into our healing process. We allow them to remind us of our worth, to hold space for us in our darkest moments, and to bring light back into our lives. Vulnerability isn't a weakness; it's the bridge that connects us to the love and support we need.

Many times, I've simply told a friend, "I'm struggling today." Whether we talked on the phone, or they told me to come over, by the time we hung up or I headed home, we were both laughing. The weight I was carrying always felt lighter after that, and I knew I was headed in the right direction.

When you stumble, remember that falling isn't failing. Give yourself the grace to feel, the courage to reach out, and the strength to keep moving forward. Because no matter how heavy today feels, brighter days are ahead. You're not alone on this path, and every step, every moment of struggle, is leading you toward something greater.

Affirmation: Every setback I face is an opportunity to rise stronger, wiser, and more determined than ever before

Journal Prompt: Think of a setback or failure you've experienced. At the time, how did it make you feel? Now, looking back, what lessons did you learn from it? How can you reframe that experience as a steppingstone toward growth and future success?

You Are Seen:

From Invisibility to Belonging

Most of my life, I felt invisible, not in the way that granted me freedom to do as I pleased, but as if I simply blended into the background, unnoticed and unmemorable. It wasn't that my parents ignored me or allowed me to run wild (though, at times, I wished they had). Rather, I felt like a wallflower, a plain Jane who made little impact on those around me. On the rare occasions when someone recognized me at the grocery store and called me by name, I was genuinely surprised. I never thought I was worth remembering, so when someone did, it caught me off guard.

In middle school and high school, I was very introverted. I had friends but I wasn't popular, only coming out of my shell around those closest to me. To this day, a few teasing incidents vividly stand out. At the time, I remember feeling embarrassed but not largely affected. I was mocked for my limited wardrobe, right down to the shoes I wore. My stepmom and dad chose not to spend their money on things they deemed luxuries, name-brand clothes and shoes included. I wanted to look nice but ended up with a closet primarily filled with the same sweatshirt in eight different colors and a few favorite pairs of jeans.

The classic all-white Reeboks my mom got me became my most prized possession. When one pair wore out, I excitedly replaced them with a new pair of the same shoe. Looking back, I realize how much those small moments shaped me. This is most likely where my current clothes addiction comes from, beginning the day I received my first paycheck from my first job. Every bit of that $5.25 per hour went to New York and Company. To this day, I buy more clothes than I need, even though I still wear the same eight favorite items daily. I mean, who doesn't need twenty different black T-shirts? It's familiar and comfortable, it's what I had growing up.

I try time and time again to experiment with bold colors and patterns but always resort to the basic color palette that feels safe. It's funny how our past lingers in the most unexpected ways.

After high school, I got married quickly. The majority of my first marriage was spent being told I only had friends because my husband had friends. He would argue and point out that no one liked me, that they liked him and therefore me by default. Though I knew it wasn't true, and have accepted it isn't true, words, especially those repeated by someone you choose to pour love into, make an impact.

The assortment of harsh words spoken for years was incredibly damaging to a fragile girl already struggling with self-esteem and confidence. No matter how many friends I made, the challenges I overcame, or the successes I had, those words were constantly reiterated, so no matter how happy I was with life or how content

I felt with my little place in the world, I still felt invisible, unmemorable, and insignificant.

I think back to moments when I felt like an afterthought. The times when I spoke up in a group and no one seemed to hear me. The times I poured my heart into something, and it went unnoticed. The times I walked into a room an felt like I was simply taking up space. But over time, something changed. As I gained more independence and built up my confidence, I became less surprised when people remembered my face or my name and would approach me. I started feeling less uncomfortable when complimented and began to open up more.

From time to time, that timid girl who still felt unsure about herself would resurface. Then one day someone said three simple words that resonated deeply and stayed with me: **"You are seen."**

Take a moment to pause, ingest these words and the depth of their meaning, and know it's true, you are seen. No matter what anyone else's advice or opinions are, what you've been through, what you're currently going through, or what the voice in your head tells you, you are seen.

What does it mean to be seen?

To truly be seen means to be recognized, understood, and accepted for who you genuinely are—without masks, pretenses, or the need to shrink yourself to fit someone else's expectations. It goes beyond mere physical presence; it's about having your emotions, experiences, and inner world acknowledged and valued.

Being truly seen means that someone notices not just what you do but who you are at your core. It's the feeling of being deeply known, your strengths, vulnerabilities, dreams, and struggles, without fear of judgment or rejection. It's about feeling safe enough to show up authentically, knowing that your truth is respected and honored.

In relationships, being truly seen fosters deep connection and trust. It's when someone listens not just to your words but to the emotions behind them, when they celebrate your victories and hold space for your pain. It's the ultimate validation, not because you seek approval, but because your existence is acknowledged in a way that affirms your worth.

To be truly seen is one of the deepest human desires, and it starts with first allowing **yourself** to see and accept **who you are.**

There is something profoundly healing about knowing you are seen. It doesn't take grand gestures or viral moments to be significant. It happens in the quiet moments, the ones where someone truly listens to you, where a friend checks in, where someone remembers your name or your favorite coffee order. It happens in the way your presence lingers in the lives of others, even when you don't realize it.

If you've ever felt invisible, know this: you are not. If you've ever doubted your worth, know this: you are enough. If you've ever wondered if anyone notices you, believe this: **You are seen.**

And please, believe it with all your heart.

Affirmation: I am worthy of being seen, known, and accepted for who I truly am. I embrace my authenticity with confidence, knowing that I am enough just as I am.

Journal Prompt: Think of a time when you felt invisible or overlooked. What emotions did that experience bring up for you? Now, reflect on a moment when you truly felt seen, valued, and accepted. What was different about that experience? What steps can you take—within yourself and in your relationships—to cultivate a greater sense of belonging in your life?

Self-Care: More Than Just a Buzzword

Since the age of eighteen, most of my jobs have been under the umbrella of human services. Working with people in the helping profession in one way or another. Self-care has been a common term in this field for decades, due to how mentally and physically draining it is to work with others and try to fix the world's problems one person at a time. The desire to help people but not always being able to, at times being taken for granted, and helping others to the point of exhaustion has a multitude of side effects. If we don't prioritize rest and recuperation and allow it to go unchecked, it leads to burnout. But many of us wouldn't have it any other way.

The importance of self-care has caught on much more widely in recent years and I am thankful for the widespread realization of its importance because, it's pretty common knowledge that you can't pour from an empty bucket. You're unable to save someone else if you are drowning. It is widely known whether you've heard a flight attendant's safety demonstration or not, that when the plane is going down, you're instructed to first put your oxygen mask on before assisting others. **You can't help the person**

sitting next to you if you can't breathe. These are things most of us know but tend to forsake in our desire to help.

The Barriers to Self-Care

Even when we know self-care is necessary, putting it into practice isn't always easy. There are external factors that get in the way, being a new parent, starting a business, moving to a new house or a new city, or being surrounded by those who constantly take without appreciation or reciprocation. However, there are also internal barriers that we don't talk about enough.

Many of us feel guilty about taking time for ourselves, as though self-care is selfish or indulgent. We live in a culture that glorifies overwork and productivity, making us believe that rest is something we must "earn" rather than a fundamental need. For some, slowing down feels uncomfortable, as though if we stop moving, we might have to sit with emotions we'd rather ignore. Others struggle with the idea of prioritizing themselves, especially caregivers, service workers, and people who are used to putting others first.

Consider this: self-care isn't selfish, it's essential. When we neglect our well-being, we don't just harm ourselves; we also become less effective in our work, less present in our relationships, and more susceptible to stress, illness, and burnout. Taking care of yourself isn't about choosing yourself over others; it's about ensuring you have the energy and clarity to show up as your best self for those around you.

Discovering What Works for You

Self-care doesn't look the same for everyone. It isn't just bubble baths and spa days (though it can be). Depending on the season of life you're in and what's been thrown your way, carving out time for yourself may be effortless or it may feel nearly impossible. Some days, it might mean being active, and other days, it might mean giving yourself permission to do absolutely nothing.

If you're unsure what self-care looks like for you, consider asking yourself:

- What activities make me feel energized vs. drained?

- When was the last time I felt truly relaxed, and what was I doing?

- Do I need quiet solitude to recharge, or do I feel better when I'm surrounded by people?

- What small things can I incorporate into my daily routine that bring me joy?

When life is good, self-care for me involves riding my bike, going to the beach, hanging out with friends, or taking a long walk while listening to music. After my husband left, self-care looked vastly different. A short walk around the block, journaling, and binge-watching *Grace and Frankie* was all I could bring myself to do, it was all I had the energy and mental capacity for, and that's okay. Self-care isn't about doing the most, it's about doing what you need in the moment.

The Long-Term Benefits of Self-Care

One of the biggest misconceptions about self-care is that it's a temporary fix, something you do once in a while when you're feeling overwhelmed. But real self-care is a long-term investment in your well-being. When practiced consistently, it doesn't just help you recover from stress, it builds resilience.

By making self-care a habit, you create a foundation for mental and physical well-being. It allows you to show up fully for your work, relationships, and responsibilities. It helps prevent burnout rather than just treating it when it happens. And most importantly, it teaches you to value yourself enough to prioritize your needs.

Think about some of the things you enjoy and write a list of those hobbies or activities. Are you someone who enjoys sun, sand, and waves, or more of a mountain person? Would you rather participate in indoor or outdoor activities? Do you prefer the peace and solitude of being alone or being surrounded by people in an energetic environment? Whatever it is that brings peace, passion, and joy into your life, be intentional about setting aside time for it. Because at the end of the day, the most valuable asset you have is **you.**

Affirmation: I honor myself by prioritizing my well-being. Taking care of myself is not selfish, it is necessary, and I am worthy of the love and care I give to others.

Journal Prompt: What does self-care mean to you? Think about the ways you currently take care of yourself—physically, mentally, and emotionally. Are there areas where you tend to neglect your own needs? Write down three small, realistic ways you can prioritize self-care this week and how you think it will impact your well-being.

The Transformative Power of Gratitude

What if I told you that the hardest moments in your life could become your greatest source of strength? It may not feel that way now, especially if you're facing heartbreak, betrayal, or loss. But what if the challenges you've endured aren't happening *to* you, but *for* you? Stay with me for a moment, I know some events in life feel unbearably tragic and unfair. Yet, no matter how painful it is, you have the power to transform those experiences into something meaningful. You can take what has impacted you and use it to empower you.

I know this mindset shift isn't easy. When I discovered my husband's affair or endured the verbal and mental abuse of my first marriage, I wasn't open to hearing that any of it was "for my benefit." I wasn't even ready to believe I would be okay. But over time, healing softened my heart, opened my mind, and revealed an inner strength I didn't know I had.

As time goes on, we begin to heal and the inner strength we possess is revealed. As this happens we're able to changing our mindset. We can go from feeling stuck, isolated, or helpless to feeling empowered, strengthened, capable, and ready to move forward with greater resilience. Two-time Triathlon World Champion Siri Lindley said in a podcast interview, "everything great in my life has come out of such struggle." When we start to see things from this point of view and are grateful for each day, we recognize how our circumstances mold us into the individuals we're meant to become. We realize the things that we once viewed as negative didn't happen to us but happened to stretch and grow us in new ways so we can become better versions of ourselves.

One of the most powerful aspects of gratitude is the shift in perspective it creates. Gratitude does not mean ignoring hardship or pretending challenges do not exist. Instead, it allows us to reframe difficulties as opportunities for growth. This shift in thinking does not happen overnight, but by consistently practicing gratitude, we train our minds to find meaning in even the most difficult circumstances. Over time, what once seemed insurmountable can become a steppingstone toward something greater.

Daily gratitude practices play a significant role in reinforcing this perspective shift. Whether it's keeping a gratitude journal, verbalizing appreciation to loved ones, or simply taking a moment each morning to reflect on what is good, these small habits accumulate into a powerful force. The more we practice gratitude, the easier it becomes to notice the blessings that surround us. Over time, gratitude transforms from a practice into a way of life.

During an annual girls' weekend trip to the mountains after learning of my husband's affair, I had a moment of clarity. I can't share too much, because "What happens at Bitter Goose Lodge, stays at Bitter Goose Lodge," but this particular trip was very different than the previous trips I had taken with my friends. Rather than engaging in the typical girls' weekend-away shenanigans, I spent this weekend reading, journaling, sitting in quiet reflection by the fire, talking quietly with my friends, and I finally realized there is freedom found in forgiveness.

Once I was able to forgive, peace came over me. I don't know who said it first, or who said it better—Rick Warren, Tony Robbins, or Ted Lasso—but "Forgiveness is a gift you give to yourself." It really is and it was then I was finally able to embrace this attitude of gratitude. I started asking myself, "What can I find to be thankful for? What are some things I can learn from this situation? How can I use this to be a better version of myself, and how can I use this to propel myself in the direction of my true destiny?"

Despite its benefits, we can struggle to cultivate gratitude due to common roadblocks. Stress, comparison, and focusing on what's lacking can cloud our ability to see the good in our lives. It's easy to fall into the trap of thinking gratitude is only for those whose lives are perfect, but in reality, gratitude is most powerful when life feels challenging. Acknowledging the small wins, even in tough times, can create momentum toward a more positive mindset. One way to break through these roadblocks is by practicing intentional gratitude, choosing to find one good thing in every day, no matter how difficult it may seem.

If you can, spend some time journaling about the things you have to be thankful for; it can be quite revealing. Journaling allows for reflection through documentation and opens the door to self-discovery. You may even surprise yourself with the insight you gain. Journal where you are, the things you're working to overcome, where you hope to be, and how you plan to get there. Once you're in a better place, you can look back and see where you've succeeded, which areas may still need some work and have insight and clarity for moving forward. It's an ongoing process.

Make a list of ten things you're grateful for. Not long ago, I tried this exercise myself, got to about seven, and stopped because I didn't know what else to put down. I had listed my family, friends, my job, things I possessed, and even a recent trip I was able to take. It was all the typical things people think of when someone asks, "What are you thankful for?", and I thought, "That's it," but the list required ten, so I had some thinking to do. I pushed on, and as I added more items to the list, the content of my list changed from things I have to the person I am. Looking back at how far I've come, the healing I've done, and how comfortable I am with myself, I am so thankful. I also discovered as I looked inward rather than outward, the things I'm grateful for poured out of me much more readily. I made my list of ten and was able to keep going.

Life-changing things begin to happen when we start discovering the power of gratitude. Changes typically start within yourself and then in the world around you. You may become more self-aware and more self-confident, fall more deeply in love with yourself. You may be able to more easily recognize your strengths and not allow others to devalue them. You may begin to desire more from life and actively pursue your heart's desires. Before you know it, you'll be on a new path, the path meant for you.

The long-term impact of gratitude is profound. Studies have shown that those who practice gratitude consistently experience lower stress levels, improved mental and physical health, stronger relationships, and an overall greater sense of well-being. Over time, gratitude rewires our brains, making positivity a default response rather than a conscious effort. It strengthens resilience, allowing us to face future challenges with a mindset that fosters growth instead of defeat. Gratitude is not just a fleeting feeling; it is a lifelong tool for cultivating joy and fulfillment.

In the end, gratitude is not just about acknowledging what we have; it's about recognizing who we are and who we are becoming. The simple act of listing ten things we are grateful for can open the door to deeper self-awareness and appreciation.

Remember, the practice of gratitude is a powerful tool for transformation. It allows us to cultivate joy and contentment in our lives, no matter the circumstances we face. So, let's embrace the opportunity to celebrate our journeys, our resilience, and the countless moments that shape us. With every list we make, we can transform our perspective and ultimately enrich our lives. What will you discover about yourself on your journey of gratitude?

Affirmation: Gratitude opens my heart to abundance. I choose to see the beauty in every moment and appreciate the blessings, big and small, that enrich my life.

Journal Prompt: Think of a challenging time in your life. How did that experience shape you? Now, list at least five things from that experience that you can be grateful for, whether it's strength gained, lessons learned, or unexpected blessings that came from it. How does shifting your focus to gratitude change the way you view that situation?

Time is Fleeting

I recently watched a Facebook reel showing a side-by-side comparison of your current self and your younger self using an AI filter. The discovery of what AI is capable of and how quickly it's evolving continues to blow my mind. As the nostalgic notes of "Forever Young" played, I found myself tearing up. The temptation to download the app and try it for myself was strong; I still might. But as I watched the faces of those in the reel, their expressions revealed the same thoughts swirling in my mind: "Where has the time gone?" The inevitable follow up questions then arise, "Did I do everything I intended with the time I had? Did I take advantage of every opportunity? Do those close to me know how much they mean to me? Is it too late to conquer some of those mountains?"

The realization that the length of time we have left diminishes as we age often brings these profound questions to the forefront. Time is fleeting. As a child, it seems we have nothing but time; summers stretch into infinity, and adulthood feels like a distant dream. However, looking back as an adult, it's a different story; the years "don't they go by in a blink," as Anthony Hopkins poignantly states in *Meet Joe Black*. Those words always resonated deeply. A reminder that the moments we cherish can slip away before we even realize it.

Now, as my kids are grown, I find myself reflecting on cherished memories. I remember moments when I felt time dragging on, convinced that I had all the time in the world before they turned eighteen and set off on their own journeys. I'd think, "It's going to take forever for them to grow up!" Yet, paradoxically, I also wished they would remain little forever. Now, as I look at them, I often chuckle, "They keep getting older, but I don't know how, because I haven't gotten any older at all!" Of course, that's not true. While I may still feel vibrant and remain active, I am indeed aging, and there's less sand in life's hourglass than there once was.

This reflection on time often invites a sense of urgency and introspection. I've learned that it's never too late to dream a new dream, set a new goal, or start over if you must. Life has a funny way of presenting us with opportunities to reinvent ourselves. It's important to remember that you might have to begin again many times throughout your life. Each time offers a chance for growth, for learning, and for rediscovering what truly matters to you.

At all stages of life, no matter how much sand is left in life's hourglass, it is vital to have a sense of purpose and something to live for. Purpose acts as our North Star, guiding us through the ebbs and flows of time. Whether it's pursuing a passion, nurturing relationships, or giving back to our communities, engaging with life's purpose can fill our days with meaning and joy.

As we move forward, let us not allow the passage of time to become a source of regret. Instead, let's embrace each moment, hold dear our connections, and pursue our dreams with fervor.

Because in the end, it's not just about how much time we have but how we choose to spend it.

Affirmation: I have enough time to create, grow, and live fully. I embrace each moment with presence and purpose, knowing that my journey unfolds exactly as it should

Journal Prompt: Reflect on how time has passed in your life, what moments felt like they lasted forever, and which ones seemed to fly by? If there were no limitations, what is one dream, goal, or passion you would pursue right now, no matter your age or stage in life? What small step can you take today to begin that journey?

Turning Disapproval into Determination

As we move forward together in the pursuit of finding what sets your soul on fire, it's important to acknowledge that opposition will arise. We all know there will be twists, turns, dips, peaks, and sometimes fiery coals to cross along the way. These trials will test your determination, cultivate your problem-solving skills, and shape your character into the person you need to become to achieve your goals.

It may come as a surprise when people, whether intentionally or unintentionally, throw stumbling blocks in your path. Naysayers and doubters exist, and sometimes they come from the people you'd least expect. You might hear comments aimed at shutting down your ideas, questioning your abilities, or planting seeds of doubt in your mind. These remarks can be subtle, disguised as concern or practicality, or they can be outright dismissive, minimizing your dreams and ambitions.

Sometimes, these voices come from strangers or acquaintances, but other times, they come from close friends, family members, or even mentors—people whose opinions you value and whose words carry weight. It can be disheartening to realize that not everyone will believe in your vision or support your journey.

Their doubt may stem from their own fears, limitations, or past experiences rather than a true reflection of your potential.

It's important to recognize that external skepticism does not define your capabilities or determine your success. The road to personal growth and achievement is often met with resistance, but that resistance can serve as fuel rather than a roadblock. Use the doubt of others as motivation to push forward, to prove to yourself—not to them—that you are capable, strong, and worthy of your aspirations. Stay committed to your path, surround yourself with those who uplift and encourage you, and remember that belief in yourself is far more powerful than the doubts of others.

Do it anyway! If you passionately believe in your path, you don't need anyone's approval. It can be tough to navigate the desire for acceptance but remember: you're following your heart for your satisfaction, not anyone else's.

They Said It Couldn't Be Done – But They Did It Anyway

History is filled with people who were told they wouldn't succeed, only to prove their doubters wrong. Consider Walt Disney, fired from a newspaper job because he was told he lacked imagination. Imagine if he had believed that and quit pursuing his dreams. Instead, he built one of the largest entertainment empires in the world.

Or take J.K. Rowling, who was rejected by 12 publishers before *Harry Potter* became a worldwide sensation. If she had listened to the naysayers, her story would have never been told. Michael Jordan, widely regarded as one of the greatest basketball players of all time, was cut from his high school basketball team. He didn't let that define him. Instead, he worked harder and turned failure into fuel.

You're not alone in facing opposition. Every great achiever has encountered doubt, rejection, and obstacles along the way. What sets them apart isn't the absence of challenges, but their refusal to let those challenges define them.

How to Overcome Opposition and Keep Moving Forward

So, what can you do when people doubt you or, when you start questioning yourself? Here are some strategies to help you push through:

1. **Cultivate a Strong "Why"** – When you deeply understand your purpose, external doubts become less powerful. Ask yourself, *why does this dream matter to me?* Write it down and revisit it when challenges arise.

2. **Filter Out Negative Voices** – Not all criticism is valid. Learn to distinguish between constructive feedback and discouragement. If someone tells you *why* something won't work, ask yourself: *Does this person have experience in what I'm pursuing? Are they offering solutions, or just negativity?*

3. **Surround Yourself with Supporters** – Seek out mentors, like-minded individuals, and those who genuinely believe in your potential. Their encouragement can help drown out negativity.

4. **Develop Resilience Through Mindset Shifts** – See challenges as opportunities for growth rather than obstacles. Every setback is a lesson that brings you closer to your goal.

5. **Use Doubt as Fuel** – Let negativity motivate you. Instead of being discouraged by naysayers, adopt a *"watch me do it"* mentality.

6. **Practice Self-Affirmation** – Negative words from others can take root if you allow them. Counteract that with positive self-talk: *I am capable. I am worthy. I am becoming the person I need to be.*

7. **Take Action Anyway** – The best way to silence doubt is through action. Keep pushing forward, even if progress is slow. Consistency beats doubt every time.

Turning Disapproval Into Admiration

At first, those who doubt you may openly express their disapproval. They may be disappointed in the choices you make, question the time you dedicate to your goals, or feel that your priorities should be different. If you're keeping things in balance with your new flow of self-care and a goal-oriented lifestyle, their negativity doesn't have to affect you.

Dare to disappoint. You cannot control how others react to your journey. Their opinions, doubts, and expectations are *not* your responsibility. Your responsibility is to yourself, your growth, your dreams, and the life you are working to build.

Here's something to consider, often, the source of others' disappointment has nothing to do with you. They may be projecting their own fears or regrets. Maybe they see you chasing something they were too afraid to pursue themselves. Their doubts may come from love but are wrapped in fear of the unknown.

Whatever the reason, your job isn't to make them comfortable, it's to keep moving forward. And here's the best part: many of those who doubt you now will eventually admire you for your persistence. As they watch you succeed, their disappointment may turn into inspiration.

The Ones Who Show Up to Cheer You On

While there will always be doubters, there will also be people rooting for you in ways you may not even realize. Some will admire you from afar, watching your journey unfold, silently gaining courage from your resilience. Others will stand by your side, offering encouragement, support, and belief in you, even on the days you struggle to believe in yourself.

Surround yourself with those people. Lean into their encouragement. And most importantly, believe in yourself even when no one else does, because the greatest victories often come after the hardest battles.

So, despite the opposition, despite the doubts, despite the stumbling blocks placed in your path... keep going. Do it anyway.

Affirmation: I am confident in my path, resilient in my pursuit, and unaffected by the doubts of others. My dreams are mine to achieve, and I will keep moving forward with courage and determination.

Journal Prompt: "Think about a time when someone doubted you or discouraged you from pursuing something important to you. How did it make you feel, and how did you respond? If you could go back, would you handle it differently? What steps can you take now to ensure that doubt, whether from yourself or others, doesn't hold you back from achieving your goals?"

The Tapestry of Friendship

Human connection is one of the most beautiful things that make life worth living. We're surrounded by people every day; they are and always will be part of our lives. Some are in your life from birth to death, and some are just passing through momentarily. Some are family, and some are friends you choose to make family. Others you may expect to be part of your life for the long haul, but it doesn't always work out that way. Some pop in and out but always happen to be there when you need them the most. One thing I believe is each of these people adds value and meaning to our lives.

Every day, we're moving in different directions with various things fighting for our attention. Sometimes, people come into our lives like a hurricane and end up being the breath of fresh air you didn't know you needed. There's value in every relationship, and each interaction is a precious moment to store in your treasure box. Some friendships may feel temporary or brief, but their significance often lasts longer than you think.

I've learned that we always seem to have exactly who we need, exactly when we need them. One friend, whom I rarely kept in touch with for over twenty years, helped me move my things hundreds of miles without hesitation or asking any questions. She was a great friend for a long time, then life happened, as it does. We became busier and went in separate directions for a while. We stayed in touch, primarily through liking each other's social media posts, and saw each other at the occasional baby shower or graduation party. Neither of us ever felt bad about drifting apart because we both understand that it happens. But our love, respect, and close bond, the kind that says, "I'm always here for you," stayed intact. And in my time of great need, she showed up without question.

This is the essence of true friendship: even when years pass or paths diverge, the foundation remains. And when those paths cross again, it feels as though nothing has changed.

The Evolving Nature of Friendship

I've discovered that friendships aren't static; they evolve just as we do. Over time, our careers, families, and personal priorities change, making it natural for some relationships to grow apart, while others grow stronger. There are friends with whom I share daily experiences, and then there are those who I may not talk to for months or even years. But when we reconnect, it's as if no time has passed.

Sometimes, friendships grow deeper over time, even when distance comes into play. I have a dear friend who I grew much closer to after I moved hundreds of miles away than when she lived just ten minutes down the road. There's something about the space and time between us that allowed our bond to strengthen in ways I never expected. It's an ironic truth that the distance sometimes truly does makes the heart grow fonder.

Friendship and Timing

There's something magical about the timing of relationships. Sometimes we meet people and think, "What are the chances we'd cross paths?" But those are the moments we later realize we needed them in our lives, even if we didn't know it at the time. A friend I lost touch with years ago now lives in the town where I currently reside. We both moved in different directions for years, but the universe had a way of bringing us back together when we needed it most.

It's amazing how life brings us the right people at the right time. The relationships we have at various points in our lives contribute to our personal growth in ways we often can't predict. Sometimes it takes years for people to enter your life, and when they do, it feels like everything that led up to that moment was meant to bring you to them.

What Makes Friendships Last

While some friendships are fleeting, others remain steadfast despite the trials of time and distance. The key to lasting friendships lies in mutual respect, communication, and shared growth. True friends understand that life happens, that change is inevitable, and that distance doesn't always equate to loss.

Here's the important part: these friendships don't just last by chance. They last because we choose to nurture them, even when life gets in the way. Whether it's a text to check in, a quick phone call, or making time for that in-person visit, the effort we put into these relationships is what keeps them strong. The best friendships are the ones where both people are willing to show up emotionally, physically, and mentally, when it counts the most.

Yes, sometimes this means being vulnerable. Asking for help, sharing your struggles, and not pretending everything is fine when it's not. It can be hard to let people see you at your weakest, but real friends want to be there for you, not just in the good times, but in the difficult moments as well. That's the beauty of vulnerability: it creates deeper, more meaningful connections.

The Gift of Vulnerability and Friendship

It's easy to put on a smile and pretend you're okay when you're not. But true friends can see through that mask and are the ones who want to help carry the load. It's important to open up and allow others to see your real self, your fears, and your struggles. This is the only way we truly connect on a deep level.

Friendships that endure aren't about perfection or having everything together. They're about being there for each other, in all our messy, imperfect, and evolving selves. The key to keeping these connections alive is honest communication, mutual support, and an understanding that life's ups and downs are part of the journey we share together.

Never discount a friend you've lost contact with or feel distant from. It's okay to grieve the changes in your friendships and the way they've evolved, but remember, the most important thing is that you have been a part of their lives, and they've been a part of yours. Even when time, distance, and change separate you, the bond you share doesn't have to fade away. And if it does, it was meant to. True friendships will always find their way back when the timing is right.

Affirmation: I cultivate friendships with love, trust, and authenticity. I give and receive support, and my connections grow stronger with kindness and understanding.

Journal Prompt: Reflect on a friendship or connection in your life that has changed over time. How has it evolved, and what role does it play in your life now? What have you learned about yourself through this relationship, and how can you nurture it moving forward

Building Meaningful Connections In A Changing World

Perhaps you're facing isolation, asking yourself "What if I have no friends? What if I'm truly one hundred percent all alone, on my own?" I've had those same thoughts and feelings and times in my life. One of the first things I did after moving was to join several community Facebook groups. There seems to be something for everyone and everything! I decided it would be a great way to learn about the town, local events, where things are located, and maybe make a few new friends. I also figured at the very least that joining a few community Facebook pages would be extremely entertaining. IYKYK (If you know, you know)!

I found myself surprised by how many posts I saw from people looking for friendship, asking where to meet others with similar interests, sharing real struggles about feeling isolated, and publicly expressing true vulnerability. What struck me most was that these were not just younger individuals or people who had just moved to town, people of all ages, from moms at home with no adult interaction to fifty-somethings seeking new connections in a rapidly changing town, were reaching out for the same thing: meaningful relationships.

The town I moved to is a salad bowl of diversity, and people everywhere are moving at lightning speed due to financial reasons, careers, proximity to beautiful beaches, or simply a desire for change, leaving familiarity, life-long friends, and family behind. Making new friends isn't easy for everyone. It can be especially challenging for young families who feel isolated by their family obligations and as we age, it can become more challenging to jump into existing friend groups. Jenny across the street no longer comes knocking on your door and asks you to come outside and play while the moving van is still unloading.

Through Facebook, I discovered there were moms seeking more adult interaction while managing busy home lives, twenty-somethings looking for friends with similar interests, and fifty-somethings looking for new ways to connect with others. So, they turned to social media to try and find connections, and you know what? Good for them for using their resources and reaching out. You can't get answers to questions you don't ask. You've heard the saying, "The only dumb question is the one not asked?" The online community rallied behind those bold enough to ask by offering suggestions on where to meet people, what to do, where to go, and even offer to meet up at the park. They were also empathetic, understanding, and encouraging. Not something you always see on social media but definitely refreshing.

The Importance of Self-Awareness in Making Connections

As you try to find new connections, it's vital to reflect on who you are, what your values are, and what you're looking for in relationships. Are you seeking someone to share your interests with? Are you looking for a friend who challenges you and helps you grow? Understanding your needs will help you meet people who align with your personal journey.

It's not just about finding anyone to fill the gap. It's about finding someone who can truly add value to your life. Consider what you enjoy, what hobbies you like, or what goals you're working towards. As you dive into these areas of interest and find outlets that support your personal growth, you're likely to meet like-minded people with similar interests and a shared life path. This mutual understanding and shared growth can lay the foundation for a connection that goes beyond just casual friendship.

Personal Growth Through New Connections

The process of making new friends is not only about finding people to share life with, but it's also about your own growth. Putting yourself out there, even when it feels challenging, is a way to build resilience and grow your capacity for connection. When you meet someone new, you are learning more about yourself, what you value, how you communicate, and how you navigate the ups and downs of relationships.

In my journey, I've learned that real friendships often test your boundaries and force you to reflect on your own behavior, your likes, dislikes, and what you want from a relationship. Friendships offer more than just companionship, they offer opportunities for growth, self-discovery, and even a chance to heal from past hurts.

And remember: making connections is not just about finding friends for yourself. It's also about offering support, empathy, and companionship to others. Many of us crave connection, and we all have the power to reach out and help someone else feel seen, heard, and valued. When you show up for others, you often find that they're more than happy to show up for you in return.

Ultimately, the goal is not just to have friends, but to experience a sense of belonging. It's about finding your "people", those who make you feel accepted and valued, despite your flaws. Real connection isn't about perfection; it's about being able to show up as your authentic self. When you experience true belonging, you feel safe to be vulnerable, to grow, and to evolve alongside others.

Your people are out there, waiting for you. Sometimes, it just takes a little courage and persistence to find them. You might not meet them in the way you expect, but when you do, it will feel like you've found your place in the world.

Affirmation: I am open to genuine connections, and the right friendships will come into my life at the perfect time.

Journal Prompt: Think about a time when you were feeling lonely or disconnected. What actions did you take to move through those feelings and open yourself up to new connections? How did it feel to take that step? Reflect on a recent connection you made with someone new. What did you learn about yourself through that interaction, and how did it contribute to your personal growth?

The People We Meet:

Purposeful Connections

I believe every person who enters our lives is allowed in for a reason. Some people stay for years, shaping us in ways we can easily recognize. Others appear briefly, yet their impact is just as meaningful. Time does not determine significance; it's the depth of the connection and the lessons they leave behind that truly matter.

Think about it: have you ever met someone who changed your perspective within minutes? Perhaps their presence brought you a sense of peace, as if they were a missing piece of calm you didn't realize you needed. Maybe they spoke a simple truth that resonated so deeply it lingered in your mind, setting off a chain reaction of self-discovery and new possibilities.

Then there are those whose impact isn't fully understood until long after they've left our lives. Like the high school teacher who tried to instill wisdom we brushed off as unnecessary. Or the friend who encouraged us in ways we only appreciated once we faced struggles they had already prepared us for. At the time, we may not have recognized their significance, but life has a way of bringing their words and actions back to us when we need them most.

As we grow, we begin to reflect on these relationships with newfound clarity. We ask ourselves: *Was this a positive connection, or was it a lesson in disguise?* Some people bring light, encouragement, and wisdom, while others challenge us in difficult ways. Either way, every connection serves a purpose.

The beauty of life is that we get to choose what we carry forward. We can hold onto the positive experiences, cherishing the lessons and the love shared. And for the painful experiences, we can take the wisdom gained and release the rest. Nothing is coincidental; every encounter is part of a greater journey.

Take a moment to reflect: Who has shaped your life in ways you didn't expect? What lessons have these connections left behind?

Because whether brief or lifelong, every person we meet has a role in our story.

Affirmation: Every relationship I encounter, whether a blessing or a lesson, shapes me into the person I am meant to become.

Journal Prompt: Who is someone who has left a lasting impact on my life, whether they were in it for a short time or many years? What did I learn from them? Are there any past connections I need to make peace with, whether by appreciating their value or releasing their hold on me? If I could send a message of gratitude to someone who changed my life, what would I say?

Finding Peace in Release

Whether accidental or intentional, none of us expect to be hurt by those we care about, but it happens, because people are imperfect. I know I've both been hurt and have hurt others, but no matter who, when, or what the circumstance, it always seems to come as a surprise to one or both parties involved. The people closest to us are often the last ones we suspect of bringing pain into our lives, but inevitably, they're the ones capable of inflicting the deepest wounds, because of how much of ourselves we pour into those relationships. If we didn't care, their words and actions wouldn't hold power. But when it's someone we trust, love, or admire, the sting of betrayal cuts deep.

It's in those moments of unexpected heartbreak that we're faced with a truth we'd rather not acknowledge: sometimes, the very people we believed would be our greatest champions are the ones who hurt us the most. The disbelief that follows, the *How could they do this to me?* or *I never thought they were capable of this*, can be just as painful as the wound itself. It's a betrayal we see echoed throughout history, even in Shakespeare's *Julius Caesar*, when he turns to his closest confidant in disbelief and utters, *"Et tu, Brutus?"*

But pain, no matter how unjust, can serve a purpose. Disappointment and hurt teach us how to stand up for ourselves, to define and enforce boundaries, and to fight for what we believe is right and true. Healing after my divorce required me to do something I had never done before, I had to speak my truth, unapologetically and without expectation.

I chose to share my feelings with the people who had hurt me the most, friends I had trusted, the husband I had loved, even the pastor who had joined us in marriage. I spoke honestly, not out of anger or retaliation, but because I needed to release what had been weighing on me. I hoped that, at the very least, they would hear me, that my words would shine a light on the impact they had made. Maybe—just maybe—they would walk away understanding that how we treat people *matters*.

But hope and reality do not always align.

Some friends offered flimsy excuses, brushing my pain aside as if it were an overreaction. Others ignored my words entirely. When I finally gathered the strength to confront my husband, my cries were met with silence. I had prepared myself for anger, for denial, for a desperate attempt to justify the choices that had led us here. But what I wasn't prepared for was *nothing*. No remorse. No apology. No reaction at all. He simply sat there, expressionless. The emptiness of his response echoed louder than any words ever could. I had given him my truth, and in return, I received silence.

So, I left.

I reached out to my pastor, the man who had counseled us before our vows, the one who had stood before us on our wedding day. I expressed my disappointment, not just in my marriage, but in *his* absence throughout its unraveling. He had been there for the beginning, but when everything fell apart, he was nowhere to be found. His response? Deflection. He took no ownership, no accountability. Instead of acknowledging my pain, he handed me a hollow, dismissive phrase: *"I'm sorry you felt let down."* A non-apology. A polite way of saying, *That's your problem, not mine.*

I wasn't expecting an apology, not really. I wasn't seeking closure from them; I had already begun finding it within myself. The moment I released what was heavy on my heart; I had already done what mattered most. Because healing isn't about whether others understand or acknowledge your pain, it's about releasing yourself from the burden of carrying it alone.

Speaking my truth wasn't about changing them. It was about freeing *me.*

I found peace not in their responses, but in letting go. I learned that closure isn't something we always receive from others; sometimes, it's something we give to ourselves. Some people will never own up to the pain they've caused, and that's okay. It is not my job to force accountability, nor is it my responsibility to hold onto the weight of their choices. What was my responsibility was making sure I released it all, that I set my boundaries, and that I walked away with my self-respect intact.

That, in itself, was enough.

Affirmation: I release the pain of the past and embrace the peace that comes with speaking my truth. My healing is my own, and I am free.

Journal Prompt: What boundaries will I put in place moving forward to protect my peace and emotional well-being? How can I give myself the closure I need, rather than waiting for it from others? What does "letting go" truly mean to me, and how will I know I've fully embraced it?

Confidence Is Contagious

Vince Lombardi once said, "Confidence is contagious, so is [a] lack of confidence." This has been scientifically proven to be one of the main reasons extremely successful entrepreneurs reach high levels of success[1]. They aren't just confident, they're overly confident. They take risks where others won't. They convince people that goals aren't just obtainable, but that failure is unfathomable. A future without their inventions, machines, mechanisms, or creative solutions is presented as a world that doesn't even make sense. Their confidence is so high and so contagious that everyone buys into what they're selling and follows without a second thought.

I thank my father for instilling the importance of confidence in me. My father, whom I haven't heard from or spoken to in over twenty years, who's never met his beautiful, amazing grandchildren, who kicked me out of the house just weeks before my high school graduation because I engaged in good, old-fashioned, typical Generation X youth shenanigans. Yes, him. I am thankful for constantly hearing, "You can do anything you set your mind to" throughout my formative years. There was no shortage of confidence building as I grew up. Although for quite a long period of time my confidence dwindled, the were planted throughout my adolescent years that I was able to water and thus began to grow once I regained my independence and surrounded myself with the right people.

For years I found myself questioning my value, but I came to realize that adversity is not just a setback; it is a powerful teacher. I had to learn how to rebuild my confidence from the ground up. Every challenge became a lesson in resilience, every hurtful situation an opportunity to prove to myself that I was capable of overcoming anything. The key was to not let the pain define me, but to use it to fuel the fire of my growth.

Thanking someone who has severed relations is another reminder that we can find something to be thankful for within the role each person played in our lives and the contributions they made, even if they're no longer an active part of our lives.

As you continue to purposely take steps towards personal growth, I encourage you to adopt this same principle because I really do believe you can do anything you set your mind to. Do you have someone telling you this same truth? If so, that's great! If not, look in the mirror and tell yourself, "I can do this." Listen to those words and make them your new mantra. Next, say the thing you have your heart set on accomplishing. Write it on a Post-it and put it on your mirror so it's the first thing you see every morning. "I can do this. I can do anything I set my mind to. I can (insert the goal you want to achieve)!"

We receive back what we put out into this world, gratitude and confidence included. Gratitude, I've learned, is not just about appreciating what you have. It is a state of mind that, when practiced daily, amplifies your confidence. When you focus on what you are grateful for, it shifts your perspective from scarcity to abundance. It teaches you to recognize your strengths, your wins, and all the moments where you've shown up for yourself. I began to make a daily habit of gratitude, whether it was acknowledging my successes, or simply being thankful for the small moments of joy that I used to overlook. This shift in mindset slowly built up my self-worth and reinforced my belief that I had what it took to achieve anything.

Put your energy toward the things you want and speak confidently over them as if they're already yours. Keep your head held high and a firm resolve—you're going to conquer the world and crush all your goals. You've got this—and it's only a matter of time!

Affirmation: I am strong, capable, and worthy. With every step I take, my confidence grows, and I embrace the power within me.

Journal Prompt: Think about a moment when you felt truly confident. What was happening in that moment, and how did it feel? What factors or beliefs contributed to your confidence? Reflect on how you can bring more of that feeling into your life now. What steps can you take to nurture and grow your confidence moving forward?

Positive Self-Talk

Growing up, my dad was really into reading books in the genre of motivational/self-help, positive thinking, and leadership. After he devoured these books, he regularly passed on the knowledge he gained from his reading to the rest of the family. At one time, our family's bookshelves were adorned with my mother-in-law's collection of Danielle Steele on one side and books written by Dale Carnegie, John Maxwell, and similar authors on the other. He loved to constantly remind us how special we were and that we could do anything we set our minds to. He also loved to constantly remind us of the power of positive thinking. I encourage you to adopt similar habits and speak to or about yourself positively.

As I mentioned previously, there was no shortage of confidence building in my childhood home. I believe that encouragement and constant positivity helped to shape my optimistic outlook, despite the many challenges I had to overcome. I believe that constructive thinking not only helped shape my outlook, but, in some ways, provided a protective barrier that I was unaware even existed during a time it was most needed. Because of this, I encourage you to speak to and about yourself positively and do this often. Not only is it important to be kind to yourself and give yourself grace, but it's also important to have the courage to believe others when they do the same, because you are worthy.

Our thoughts shape our reality, and our words reinforce our thoughts. This is why positive language is so impactful. When we speak positively to ourselves, we create a ripple effect that influences not only our own behavior but also how others perceive us. The language we use, whether internal or external, affects our self-esteem, our confidence, and our actions.

For example, think about the phrase "I can do this." It's a declaration of empowerment. When you say this out loud or silently to yourself, you're affirming that you have the capability to handle challenges and succeed. Positive language creates a cycle of affirmation that reinforces your belief in yourself and your abilities.

In contrast, negative language, such as "I can't" or "I'm not good enough," weakens our self-image and prevents us from stepping into our full potential. When you repeatedly tell yourself "I can't," you solidify a narrative of failure before you've even begun. Negative language not only limits your opportunities but also drains your energy and enthusiasm.

The impact of positive language extends beyond self-talk. It affects how you communicate with others. People who speak positively about themselves and their abilities often inspire others to do the same. They attract people who believe in them and support their growth. Positive language fosters connection, trust, and encouragement. It creates an environment where growth is not just possible but inevitable.

What does your inner dialogue tell you daily? Does it inspire you to believe in yourself and your abilities? Does it build your confidence and encourage you to reach your full potential? Most importantly, are you able to recognize if your thoughts are positive or self-critical? Ask yourself, "Would I say these things to my best friend?" "Would I say these things to my child?" or "How would I feel if someone else talked to me like this?" If your thoughts toward yourself are not something you would say to encourage another or find encouraging from someone else, take a moment, pause, and turn any negatives into positives one thought at a time.

As the saying goes, "You are the company you keep." The same can be said of your thoughts: "You are the thoughts you think." Phrases I often heard during my formative years include, "You can do anything you set your mind to," "Dream big," and "Can't isn't a word." My dad never allowed the word "can't" in our home. Any time I said it, he would make me repeat the sentence, reframe it, and replace "can't" with "can." Very annoying to a fourteen-year-old, but it's an impactful practice, and so very true.

Saying "I can't" is also a difficult habit to break once stuck in that mindset. I know this due to how many times I was stopped in my tracks to repeat and reframe my sentences. "I can't," is essentially equivalent to: "I won't," "Why bother?" or "Don't even try, because you'll fail." When you say, "I can," you give yourself the permission and motivation to take steps forward, to try, to give it a go and see what happens. Maybe you'll make a mistake or two before being successful, but each time you'll learn, tell yourself "I can do this," and try again. Eventually, you'll succeed because you keep telling yourself you can until there's no room for doubt. Saying "can't" will hold you back. Saying "can" will propel you forward. I learned how to do a lot of things using the word "can" that I may not have otherwise invested time in learning.

The "I can" vs. "I can't" belief system is more than just a matter of semantics—it's the lens through which we view our world and our potential. By shifting from "I can't" to "I can," we open ourselves up to new opportunities and possibilities. Positive language acts as the fuel for this mindset shift, empowering us to take action, overcome challenges, and step into our full potential.

You are the words you speak. The language you use, both in how you talk to yourself and others, has the power to shape your future. So, today, choose to say, "I can," choose to speak positively, and watch as you begin to create the life you've always dreamed of.

Affirmation: My words have power, and I choose to speak to myself with kindness, confidence, and unwavering belief in my worth.

Journal Prompt: Reflect on a recent challenge you faced. How did your inner dialogue influence your actions and emotions during that time? What negative thoughts did you have, and how could you reframe them into positive affirmations? Write down at least three positive statements about yourself that you can use in future moments of self-doubt or struggle.

A Growth Mindset

I did things a little unconventionally when carrying out my "success sequence" in life. Society often promotes a specific 'success sequence', graduate, go to college, get a good job, get married, and then have kids. But life doesn't always unfold in a linear way, and that's okay. My journey was unconventional, but I wouldn't change it because it led me to exactly where I needed to be. I graduated high school, fell in love, started a family, and then decided I wanted to go to college and continue my education. When I graduated high school, I didn't know what I wanted out of life or what I wanted my future to look like. My friends and those I graduated high school with all seemed to have their paths laid out before them, but I needed a gap year—time to figure out what I was truly passionate about and how to get from where I was to where I wanted to be. It took a while to figure it out, but when I did, I was adamantly ready.

My husband opposed my desire to further my education. I recall asking on various occasions before starting a family his thoughts on my attending school, taking classes, and furthering my education as I began to crave a more specific future, and the answer was always the same. Simply no. So, I was forced to get creative when I began college. Before it became popular and common, I enrolled in online college courses. When online college classes were first introduced, many didn't believe an online degree was equivalent to a "real education." But I longed to learn and grow, and I believed in myself, so I took the plunge. I hid my classes from my husband for months, working secretly during the day while he was at work and the kids took their naps. Inevitably all things done in darkness come to light and one day my sister-in-law accidentally spilled the beans. He wasn't happy, we argued, but eventually, he got over it when he realized I was all in and that wasn't going to change. I was proud that I stood up for myself and what I believed would be best for my future.

While in college, not only did I learn the subject matter of the classes I attended, but I also learned that gaining knowledge about something you love or are passionate about comes more easily than those subjects we are not interested in. If lifelong learning were a career, I would happily dedicate my life to it. The joy of expanding my knowledge has always driven me forward. People would often ask how I juggled all the things on my plate, but I never felt like I had a good answer because to me, it never felt like juggling, it was simply a priority I embraced wholeheartedly. I graduated with my master's degree over ten years ago and I'm still learning. While I no longer have the desire to return to a formal classroom, my passion for learning hasn't faded. As I set new goals and work to achieve them, I immerse myself in that subject so I can accelerate my movement forward.

To begin writing this book, I started going to a writing group, listening to podcasts, reading books on writing, and surrounding myself with like-minded people to educate myself from their experiences.

Looking back, I realize that my determination to pursue education was about so much more than a degree. It was about reclaiming my identity and choosing growth over stagnation. If I could tell my younger self one thing, it would be this: "You are capable of more than you realize, and no one has the right to put a limit on your potential." Every new piece of knowledge felt like a steppingstone toward a brighter, more independent future. Learning wasn't just about earning a degree, it was about proving to myself that I was capable, that I could redefine my own path. Education became my quiet rebellion, my declaration that I was in control of my future.

Embrace this mindset of growth. Every time you set a new goal or have something you are intentionally working toward, immerse yourself in learning everything you can about it and keep fueling that fire. Surround yourself with like-minded people who are passionate about that same goal, read about it, research it, talk about it, and engage in activities supporting it. Not only will you learn about your passion, but you'll grow in knowledge and increase your confidence, the new force to keep propelling you forward! An additional bonus is that you'll meet and make friends with similar interests.

Affirmation: I am constantly learning, evolving, and growing, every challenge is an opportunity to become a stronger, wiser version of myself.

Journal Prompt: Think of a time when you faced a challenge that initially felt impossible. How did you push past self-doubt, and what did you learn about yourself in the process? What is one area of your life right now where you can apply that same resilience and belief in your ability to grow?

Challenge Yourself

In high school, I was the girl with a seventeen-minute mile. I know; sadly, I didn't even try. When I did try to run on those dreaded mile-run gym class days, my thighs would become incredibly red and itchy, and I felt like I couldn't breathe. I would be so uncomfortable I thought something must be wrong with me. I'd slow down and walk around the track, frustrating my gym teacher and making my class wait. Running was not in my blood. For years, I accepted the idea that I just wasn't meant to be an athlete. I never imagined that decades later, I'd be voluntarily lacing up running shoes.

Fast forward almost twenty-five years. Seeking a healthy outlet post-divorce, I found it in various forms of exercise. I tried Zumba, POUND class, kickboxing, and even began running. Eventually, I ran regularly and loved it, signing up for races, texting my running buddy daily about how far we planned to go or what path we wanted to take, and spending entirely too much money on running shoes. Running taught me discipline, perseverance, and how to push through discomfort, lessons that extended far beyond fitness.

If you're a runner, kudos to you! I love running. If you're not a runner, I don't blame you, running sucks. I'd much rather run to the refrigerator for more queso. I have a love/hate relationship with running, and if you're a runner too, you've probably felt the same way at one point or another. I avidly ran for a while, stopped, then began running again. But when I moved to North Carolina, where the humidity feels like a wet blanket at dawn, I told myself I was done with running. And yet... part of me still misses it. Kind of. Maybe. See what I mean? It's a love/hate dynamic.

Through this exploration, I've come to realize we can do far more than we think if we challenge ourselves. Set a goal for yourself and set it big, because you can achieve it! Most often, the things holding us back are ourselves, our fears, and our perception of what our limitations might be.

Imagine if you had no limitations. Imagine having childlike enthusiasm and not even knowing what the word "limitation" is. Now, approach life with that same fearless enthusiasm, that you can do anything and nothing can hurt you. I'm not suggesting you dive into the deep end without knowing how to swim, but enthusiastically and fearlessly pursue your dreams. In doing so, you may have to do some things that take you outside of your comfort zone.

When you reach new milestones, challenge yourself to keep going, don't shy away or turn back. Remind yourself that you can do this, even if you're fearful or anxious, do it anyway. I never thought I could be a runner, but I became one. And if I could push past my own self-imposed limits, what else am I capable of? What else are **you** capable of?

Being taken out of our comfort zone and challenged to go beyond ourselves is how we build character. You will astonish yourself when you see what you are made of and what you can achieve. Each broken-down barrier will build your confidence until it shines so brightly others can see it. You'll learn things about yourself you didn't know before. You'll feel what it's like to excel, and it'll cause you to crave continual success.

Affirmation: I am capable, strong, and ready to rise to any challenge—because I believe in myself and my limitless potential.

Journal Prompt: Think about a time when you accomplished something you initially thought was beyond your abilities. What motivated you to keep going? How did it feel when you succeeded? Now, identify a current goal that challenges you. What steps can you take to push past any doubts or fears and move closer to achieving it?

Who's Your Toughest Critic

If someone says, "I like your nails," "What a pretty dress," or "Your hair looks nice," what is your immediate response? If your dress has pockets, the obvious response is, "Thanks, it has pockets!" But sometimes, it can be hard to receive a compliment. Especially on those days when we're struggling. Many of us tend to look in the mirror and focus on those areas we feel need improvement, while friends look at us and see only the beautiful person they know on the inside and out, and strangers might look at us and see the things that are to be admired. For some reason, we have the habit of being our own harshest critic. The things we perceive as flaws most others are entirely blind to.

Why Do We Criticize Ourselves So Harshly?

Often, our self-criticism comes from deeper places than we realize. For many of us, these harsh judgments are shaped by the expectations society places on us. The media tells us how we should look, how we should act, and what "perfect" is supposed to be. If we don't meet these external standards, we internalize the idea that we're somehow not enough. Our culture also teaches us to focus on the negative, it's easier to remember the one critical comment someone made than all the positive feedback. This negativity bias can lead us to obsess over minor flaws, while we overlook all the things that make us whole and beautiful.

Let's remember: No one is perfect. I'm certain everyone has at least one thing they'd change about themselves if they could. For example, my tummy isn't perfectly flat, I have a discolored tooth, and I wish I could be better at putting myself out there without fearing what other people might think. Well, my tummy will never be perfectly flat, after two kids, I proudly sport the multitude of stretch marks. I constantly whiten my teeth, but root damage from flying over bicycle handlebars in the third grade made its discoloration permanent and prominent (mostly to only myself). As far as putting myself out there, I strive to do better with this daily.

Through insecurity and self-consciousness, we may amplify and project our fears that someone will notice these things and unfairly judge us, but no one notices these things as much as we do. Most of the time, the people around us see us as a whole, complex person, not the isolated "imperfections" we fixate on.

The Role of Self-Talk in Personal Growth

We have the power to reframe how we see ourselves. Self-talk plays a huge role in our self-perception. Instead of thinking, "I wish I could change this about myself," we can reframe that thought to something more positive: "I accept this about myself, and I'm proud of what makes me uniquely me." Self-love and self-acceptance aren't about ignoring our growth opportunities, they're about recognizing that we're worthy of love and kindness *as we are*. From this place of acceptance, personal growth can happen without the pressure of striving for "perfection." True growth happens when we first accept ourselves as we are, which makes it easier to evolve without the fear of failure or judgment.

Embracing Self-Compassion and Spreading It to Others

As we work on accepting ourselves, we begin to influence those around us. When we're kind to ourselves, we're also able to be kinder to others. Complimenting someone else, giving them a chance to feel that same confidence you're learning to embrace, can have a ripple effect. Imagine the world we'd create if everyone embraced their imperfections and celebrated the beauty in others, too. Compliments create connection, lift spirits, and remind us of the good that exists in ourselves and the people around us. When we express appreciation, we not only raise others' confidence, but we also strengthen the bonds between us.

Today, I challenge you to catch yourself when self-criticism arises and replace it with self-compassion. Notice how this changes your perspective and your interactions with others. Be mindful of your self-talk and remind yourself, "I am beautifully born. I accept myself completely and unconditionally, and I'm continually working to be better, stronger, wiser, and the best version of me I can be." Allow yourself to be proud of how far you've come, not just where you still wish to go. And the next time someone compliments you, smile, say "thank you," and accept their words without hesitation. In that moment, you are validating yourself, and in turn, empowering others to do the same.

Affirmation: I choose to be kind and compassionate with myself, recognizing my worth and progress, rather than focusing on perfection.

Journal Prompt: Think about a recent compliment you received. How did you respond to it, and how did it make you feel? Now, reflect on a part of yourself that you often criticize or feel insecure about. Write about why this part of you is important, how it contributes to your unique story, and how you can show more kindness and acceptance toward it moving forward. How can you reframe your self-talk to embrace your imperfections as part of what makes you beautifully you?

Broken Compass

How do you keep pushing forward when you don't know which way to go? For most of my adult life, I knew exactly what I wanted to do. When I started having kids, my strongest desire was to be a stay-at-home mom. This was not an option, though, I was determined to do whatever was needed to stay home with them while still earning an income. I chose to create in-home childcare and was blessed to work with great families who had wonderful kids I could care for during the day. It provided the income I needed and gave me the ability to stay home. Not only was it the perfect situation, but as it turns out, I also felt like I'd found my life's calling; I loved it. As time went on, my dreams got bigger. I was still satisfied with watching kids in my home, but I longed to grow and make a greater impact in our community. I saw and heard there was a need and knew I could be the person to fulfill it, so I began the process of opening a small childcare center in our little town.

Over time, the business grew, I opened a second center and eventually combined the two to make one large childcare center.

I loved every minute of it—the hard work, the research, the investment of time, and especially the day-to-day operations of interacting with the children and their families. But not everything is meant to last forever. The center started costing more to operate—as many expanding businesses do. Expenses and taxes increased, but as the bills and invoices stacked up, the income did not grow to match the costs. I detested the idea of continually increasing the rates as the cost of childcare can be a heavy burden to many families. Eventually, after running in the red for as long as we could, I made the difficult choice to let it go. I knew it was the right thing to do even though, for the very first time in years, I didn't have any idea what to do next. I was at a complete loss, and I felt lost. I could live off the income from the sale of the center, but that wouldn't be sustainable long-term.

As time went on, I joked about enjoying "early retirement" when meeting friends for lunch or for an afternoon of coffee and crafts. I knew these relaxing days would come to an end but had no idea what that would look like or when it would happen. I didn't know what I wanted to do, didn't feel a calling or led in any direction, and no opportunities were presenting themselves. No doors seemed to be opening.

So, what do you do when you feel lost and without direction, when you have a restless, internal stirring you cannot shake, and you search for answers only to keep coming up empty? This is what I like to call "the waiting period." It's an in-between time or place in our lives, a temporary placeholder. One chapter has come to an end, the next chapter has yet to begin. We have no idea what's going to be written and every time we pick up the pen writers block sets in.

Waiting requires patience, but that doesn't mean we have to be passive. One day at a time, you wake up each morning and you keep going. Do what you can with each day, intentionally making the most of it. Strive to be the best version of yourself by helping others where you can, doing what you can, and talking to those whose paths cross yours. Stay positive, remain confident, and remind yourself this is just one of life's seasons, and seasons pass, so this time of waiting will also pass. Things have a way of working themselves out until our path becomes clear. During this time of unassured wandering, there are lessons to be learned here as well. Focus intently on your personal growth, take time to meditate and look inward, pray, journal, or go for walks in nature. Maintaining your forward direction is key, and what's meant for you will find its way to you in time, at the right time.

During my time of uncertainty, while brainstorming copious ideas and applying for jobs, I assisted in taking care of my then mother-in-law, who had dementia. Looking back, I treasure the moments spent with her. It was summer and pleasant enough weather that I was able to take her to do things she enjoyed while she could still enjoy them, trips to the pet store to look at the kittens and out for ice cream, lots of ice cream.

I also aided my husband with his business, and one day someone came in and began talking about a job at a company he knew was hiring. Without hesitation I gave the customer my resume and a few weeks later I was employed doing a job I loved. Throughout my time of wandering, I kept a forward movement. I did what I could to add meaning to my life and my new purpose found its way to me

Affirmation: I trust that the right opportunities will unfold at the perfect time, and I have the strength and wisdom to embrace whatever comes next.

Journal Prompt: Think about a time in your life when you felt lost or uncertain about your next steps. How did you navigate that period? What lessons did you learn during that time of waiting? Reflect on the ways you maintained forward movement, even without a clear direction. What small actions can you take today to stay positive and keep moving toward your next chapter, even if you don't have all the answers yet?

We Can't Have It All At Once

It often feels like anything we could ever imagine is within reach. Many places offer abundant opportunities, but my dad always reminded us of the importance of living within our means. He taught us to buy only what we could afford and to avoid the trap of comparing ourselves to others, after all, everyone's journey is unique. When you shift your focus to gratitude and contentment rather than what you lack, the pressure to compete with others fades away.

The constant mixed messages we receive in our everyday lives are what make things confusing. We're encouraged to spend time and money on the things we want and desire. "Treat yourself," "You deserve that," "Buy the thing," "Book the trip," "YOLO!" Then a few moments later, we're encouraged to be content with what we have and where we are, learn how to declutter to live a more minimalist lifestyle, and save for retirement. I know my brain hurts, and just like Veruca Salt, sometimes I want it all, and I want it now.

While I believe you can have it all, you can do it all, and you can achieve it all, I also believe there is a time and a season for everything. A time to spend, and a time to save. A time to plan, and a time to chase. A time to prepare, and a time to act. You can have it all, but typically not all at one time.

"Seasons" of Life

There's wisdom in knowing that each phase of life calls for different priorities, strategies, and actions. Life is full of seasons, some full of growth, some of rest, some of action, and others of reflection. The challenge lies in knowing when you're in a season of preparation versus a season of action. For example, when I was raising my kids, running a business, and going to school, it was a season of focus and expansion. But moving to North Carolina was a dream I had held onto for over twenty years, something I daydreamed about but didn't actively pursue because the timing wasn't right. When the opportunity presented itself, I recognized it was the right moment to move.

Seasons of life require patience and wisdom. It's about knowing when to move and when to wait. It's important to recognize when it's time to go after what we want, and when it's time to step back, plan, and reflect. Some moments call for bold action, leaping toward our dreams despite uncertainty, because the perfect time may never come. Other times, it's important to be mindful of the "right time," understanding that preparation and patience are just as crucial as execution. Recognizing that "right time" is key to managing our dreams and desires effectively.

The mixed messages we get from society are enough to make anyone feel like they're being pulled in a dozen directions at once. We hear messages to indulge ourselves, yet also to be minimalist and save for the future. How do we reconcile these competing messages? The answer lies in balance and timing.

It's not about rejecting either side of these messages, but about recognizing the season you're in. Are you in a season where you can focus on self-care and indulgence, or are you in a season where sacrifice and hard work are necessary for your future success? Understanding the balance between instant gratification and delayed gratification is crucial in managing our desires and making wise decisions.

One of the most important lessons I've learned is that while dreams are important, they often require time to come to fruition. The dream of opening my own business, for instance, was not a decision I made overnight. It was something I spent years thinking about. I took time to ponder the idea, to envision what it would look like, how it would function, and whether I was truly ready to take the leap. I realized that when a dream or desire continues to flourish and grow in your heart, it's something you should pursue.

The Power of Long-Term Dreams

Sometimes we hold onto dreams for years before they're realized. My desire to move to North Carolina had been with me for over twenty years. I thought about it often, unsure if it would ever come true. But when the opportunity finally came, I was ready to embrace it. Dreams that seem far off or impossible don't lose their power, they only grow stronger, like seeds waiting for the right moment to bloom. Holding onto that "someday" dream, knowing it's there and could eventually become a reality, keeps us going. Keep trusting that the right time will come. It's not about rushing to get everything at once but about waiting for the season when your efforts align with your goals.

Creating Your Own Seasons of Growth

You are in control of how you approach your dreams and how you manage your desires. Life is not a race, and it's not about comparing your progress to others. It's about recognizing where you are, what you want to achieve, and how you can honor the seasons of your life. Take time to reflect on what season you're in right now, are you in a season of growth, preparation, rest, or action? The key is to remain open to the possibilities, to stay flexible, and to trust that, in time, your path will unfold.

Affirmation: I trust the timing of my life. I am open to the flow of each season, knowing that every phase brings growth, wisdom, and opportunity. I embrace each step of my journey with patience and confidence.

Journal Prompts: Think about a dream or goal you've held onto for a long time. Where are you in your journey toward it? Is this a season of action, preparation, or patience? How can you honor this season while still keeping your dream alive?

Busyness

Take a moment to self-reflect and ask yourself, "Is my overcommitment holding me back?" Oftentimes, what keeps us from reaching our full potential is not external obstacles, but ourselves, the way we allow distractions, obligations, and unnecessary tasks to pull us in multiple directions, keeping us from focusing on what truly matters. Life presents us with responsibilities daily, but how often do we allow ourselves to become needlessly busy, mistaking constant motion for real progress?

Even as I write these words, I set a goal to be intentional, purposeful, and focused on exercising my passion, writing. Yet, I check my phone multiple times, waiting for news, only to become engrossed in something trivial. Weeks later, when I reread what I've written, that unnecessary distraction is already forgotten. But the time I lost? That's something I won't get back.

In today's world, distractions are everywhere. We are surrounded by things that keep us feeling busy, but at the end of the day, they aren't truly productive. Overcommitment, especially to things that don't align with our values and goals, doesn't just steal our time, it drains our energy, clouds our priorities, and can leave us feeling exhausted and unfulfilled.

It's easy to believe that being busy equates to being successful, but the truth is, constantly being in motion without direction is one of the quickest ways to experience burnout. I know this because I've lived it. There was a time when I felt obligated to say **yes** to everything, to every request for help, every activity, every extra task, because when you say "yes" once, the requests keep coming. As a people pleaser, I feared that if I said "no", people's opinion of me would change.

But that mindset took a toll. I found myself exhausted, stretched too thin, and emotionally drained, so busy meeting obligations that I no longer had time for things that truly mattered to me. The more I overcommitted, the more resentment I felt. I wasn't just tired; I was mentally overwhelmed. And that's when I realized: saying yes to everything meant saying no to myself.

We don't often realize it, but overcommitment can rob us of joy, creativity, and peace of mind. It's why some people struggle with rest, they feel guilty slowing down, as if productivity is the only measure of worth. But true fulfillment doesn't come from being constantly busy; it comes from being intentional with your time.

Living with Intention: Setting Boundaries for a More Meaningful Life

Instead of just reducing busyness, strive to start making intentional choices that create a more fulfilling and purpose-driven life. When my kids were young and started showing interest in sports, I made the decision that they could play **one** sport or join **one** activity at a time. I saw other families with multiple children juggling countless commitments, running from one practice to another, barely catching their breath before heading to the next thing. That was not the life I wanted for us.

I didn't want to keep up with that pace. I refused to trade peace for chaos just to meet some invisible standard of what I "should" be doing. So, I placed firm boundaries on our schedule, not because I didn't want my kids to experience different activities, but because I wanted our time together to be meaningful, not rushed.

That decision made all the difference. I wasn't overwhelmed, I wasn't constantly rushing from place to place, and I didn't care what other parents thought. Our family functioned better because I made an intentional choice about where to focus our time and energy.

Overcoming the Guilt of Saying No

For many of us, the hardest part of setting boundaries isn't deciding what to cut out, it's dealing with the guilt that comes afterward. It's easy to feel selfish when you decline an invitation, step down from a commitment, or refuse to take on more than you can handle. But here's something important to remember: Saying no doesn't mean you're lazy, setting boundaries doesn't mean you're unhelpful, and prioritizing yourself doesn't mean you don't care about others. When you say no to something that doesn't fit into your life, you're actually saying yes to something that does.

If you have little ones in public school or belong to a church, you might know the ongoing joke: "Don't say yes to volunteering unless you're ready to always be asked!" Many of us who enjoy helping struggle with saying no because we feel like we should step up. But sometimes, stepping back is just as important.

Consider this: your "yes" is someone else's "no." Every time you take on something that doesn't align with your priorities, someone else misses the opportunity to step into that role, someone for whom it might be the perfect fit. The next time you're feeling obligated to say yes, ask yourself: *Does this align with my goals right now? Do I truly want to do this, or do I feel pressured? Am I saying yes out of fear of disappointing someone?*

If it doesn't fit into your life at this moment, give yourself grace to say, *"This isn't a good time for me, but please keep me in mind for the future."* You don't have to justify your decision, and you certainly don't owe anyone an apology for protecting your time.

You Get to Decide What's Best for You

At the end of the day, you are in control of how you spend your time. Maybe that means setting limits on screen time, cutting back on extra commitments, or restructuring your daily routine to prioritize what truly matters. Maybe it means learning to say no with confidence. Whatever it is, remember this:

Busyness is not a badge of honor. Productivity isn't about how much you do, it's about what you do with purpose.

Affirmation: I am in control of my time and choose to focus on what truly matters. I prioritize my energy wisely and create space for the things that bring me peace, purpose, and growth.

Journal Prompt: What keeps you unnecessarily busy? What boundaries do you need to put in place to ensure that your time is spent on things that align with your goals and values?

Procrastination

If procrastination were a sport, I'd be a world champion with a collection of gold medals. My biggest shortcoming? The ability to put things off until the last possible second. Without deadlines, most of the important things in my life wouldn't get done in a timely manner. If I had it my way, and no external pressure, there'd be an endless cycle of scrolling through social media reels, getting snacks, lying on the couch thinking about everything I should be doing, checking my phone again, and then deciding to go for a walk because it's a nice day.

While I'm out, I might get inspired to be productive, but by the time I'm home again, I'll most likely restart the cycle. And that cycle? It usually ends with me feeling guilty for putting off things I actually want (and need) to accomplish.

I know how good it feels to be productive. On the days when I finally get my act together and cross things off my to-do list, I feel amazing. If someone asks how my day was, I over-excitedly say, "It was great!" because let's be real, productive days are great days. They just don't happen as often as I'd like.

Why Do We Procrastinate?

I know why **I** do. Hold on—let me check my phone first...

Okay, procrastination looks different for everyone, but for most of us, it boils down to a few key reasons. First, we'd rather be doing something else. Scrolling TikTok is a lot more fun than paying bills and sometimes we need to engage in mindless activity. Second, perfectionism holds us hostage. If we don't believe something will turn out perfectly, we hesitate to start at all. Third, we use procrastination as a coping mechanism. When a task feels overwhelming, our brain convinces us that ignoring it is better than facing the stress head-on. Fourth, we tell ourselves there's still time. If the deadline isn't today, the project gets pushed off, until suddenly, it is today, and panic sets in. Lastly, we wait for motivation, "I'll do it when I feel motivated," we say, but motivation is unreliable.

Sound familiar? If so, not to worry, you're not alone. The good news is that procrastination doesn't have to control your life or keep you from reaching your goals. It just requires some strategy (and a little self-discipline).

How to Overcome Procrastination (Even When You Don't Feel Like It)

If you tend to put things off like I do, the first step is self-awareness, figure out *why* you procrastinate. Once you do that, you can start implementing strategies to push past it. Here are some game changers:

One of the biggest myths about productivity is that we need to feel motivated before we start. The reality? Action creates motivation, not the other way around. Once you take the first step, momentum kicks in. One effective strategy to combat procrastination is the Two-Minute Rule—if a task takes less than two minutes, do it immediately. If it takes longer, break it into smaller chunks and start with just two minutes. More often than not, once you begin, you'll keep going.

Another powerful technique is Time Blocking & Habit Stacking. Time blocking involves scheduling tasks like appointments, setting a specific time for when you'll work on them to ensure they get done. Habit stacking, on the other hand, involves attaching a procrastinated task to something you already do daily. You could decide, *"After I make my morning coffee, I will write for five minutes."* This small adjustment helps integrate productivity seamlessly into your routine.

When tackling your to-do list, it's tempting to start with easy tasks first, but beginning with the hardest task (AKA "eating the frog") makes the rest of your day feel easier. By completing your most dreaded task early, you gain a sense of accomplishment that fuels further productivity, and it really does feel good to get the hard part overwith.

Having an accountability partner is another great way to stay on track. Find someone who will check in on your progress regularly. Knowing that someone will ask about your goals keeps you accountable. No one wants to show up to a meeting with their accountability partner and admit they haven't made progress. That trusted friend or loved one will not only check in but also serve as your cheerleader, challenging you to keep going, encouraging you to stay aligned with your goals, and will push you forward even when the road gets rough.

Lastly, reward yourself for a job well done. Make progress and productivity more enjoyable by knowing there is a reward at the end. When you make productivity feel satisfying you're more likely to stay consistent.

Give Yourself Grace—But also, a little push.

At the end of the day, we're all human. There will be times when we fall into old procrastination habits, and that's okay. The goal isn't perfection, it's progress.

Today:
Pick one thing you've been putting off and take the first small step today. No overthinking. No waiting for the "right time." Just start.

You've got this.

Affirmation: I take action with confidence and clarity, knowing that progress matters more than perfection. I am in control of my time, and I choose productivity over procrastination.

Journal Prompt: Think about a task or goal you've been putting off. What are the reasons behind your procrastination? Is it fear, perfectionism, overwhelm, or something else? Now, break that task into small, manageable steps and write down the very first action you can take today to move forward.

Trust Yourself

No one knows you better than you know yourself. Your innermost thoughts, fears, hopes, and dreams, sure, you may share some of these with those closest to you, those whom you trust. But it wouldn't surprise me if there are also things so uniquely you or so deeply personal that you choose to keep them hidden away, locked inside your heart. These are the things that, if shared, others might not fully understand the depth of their meaning, the weight they carry, or why they matter so much to you.

Trust yourself to make the right decisions and do the right thing. You'll feel it when the timing is right. You'll know when you're on the right path, and when you need to step back, regroup, and shift directions. Eventually, your head and heart will align, but even before they do, that gut feeling—that little voice inside—will whisper what you need to hear. The real challenge is not in having intuition, but in trusting it.

I remember a time when I didn't listen to my intuition, and I paid for it. The relationship I stayed in far longer than I should have. From the beginning, something felt off—small red flags, tiny nudges from within telling me, *This isn't right.* I convinced myself I was overthinking, that my gut feeling wasn't enough of a reason to walk away and there were more reasons to stay than to leave. I ignored the voice inside and stayed far longer than I should have. Looking back, I knew. I *always* knew. But I chose not to listen.

Maybe you've felt the same. Maybe there was a job opportunity you turned down, only to realize later that it could have been the perfect fit. Or there was a time you felt compelled to reach out to a friend, but you dismissed it, only to learn later they were struggling in silence. Maybe you've quieted your own instincts because you were afraid of making the wrong choice, when, deep down, you had the right answer all along. One difficulty in trusting yourself is overcoming the fear of being wrong. It's easy to second-guess, to let doubt creep in, to let outside opinions drown out your inner voice. Consider this, even if you make mistakes, you are still the best person to decide what is right for you. Every time you listen to your intuition and follow through, you build a stronger relationship with yourself.

What if, instead of questioning yourself, you started leaning in? What if, instead of silencing your inner voice, you let it guide you? You know when something isn't meant for you and you know when something feels right.

You know what's right for you and what's wrong for you. You know when you're about to do something you aren't supposed to, and how you'll feel if you do it anyway. You know when you're supposed to do something, and how it feels when you listen to the voice inside you and do it. You know when you're about to send a text you should probably delete, and how you'll feel if you send it anyway. You know when you should check in on someone you haven't talked to in a while, and you know how you feel when you ignore that inkling and don't reach out. It's that little voice within us that doesn't go away; it's there until you either listen to it or ignore it for so long that the moment is gone. I think you'll also find that if you ignore that voice for too long, the end of that road is where we find regret. That's why it's so important to listen to that inner voice—trust your gut, your intuition, that constant banter in your head that won't let something go—because it's pointing you in the direction you need to go.

The more you trust yourself, the more confident you'll become in the choices you make.

Trust your gut. Trust your instincts. Trust *you*.

No one knows you better than you do.

Affirmation: My intuition is wise and trustworthy. I confidently listen to my inner voice and trust that it will guide me in the right direction.

Journal Prompt: Think of a time when you listened to your intuition and it led you in the right direction. How did it feel to trust yourself? Now, think of a time when you ignored your gut instinct—what was the outcome? What can you learn from these experiences about trusting yourself moving forward?

Your Destiny Exists Within

Guilt washes over me when I feel like I'm talking someone into spending money they don't want to spend or into buying something they don't want or need. Being a salesperson is not a talent I was given, so I've always shied away from those types of professions, and even farther away from multi-level marketing opportunities, it's just not where I shine. Math was my favorite subject until it got too difficult to understand and Excel is overwhelming. As self-aware as I am about my shortcomings, I also know where my strengths lie: child development, helping professions, organization, communication, listening, and encouragement. Those are also things I'm passionate about and feel confident putting effort into continually developing.

If I had gone into car sales or accounting, maybe I would've been able to financially survive, but I'm not sure I would have thrived. Going to work would feel like going to work. I certainly wouldn't be happy in the long run, and I may not have been successful because of that. I might've failed miserably due to a lack of interest in my career, thinking of myself as a failure. In reality, failure in this case wouldn't be a reflection of my abilities or intelligence; it would simply be a misalignment. When we force ourselves into roles that don't match our natural skills and passions, it's no surprise when we struggle or feel unfulfilled. True success isn't just about surviving in a career, it's about thriving in one that aligns with who we are at our core.

This is what I mean when I say your destiny is already inside you. Start with what you know to be true about yourself. Maybe you love cars, math, accounting, helping others, fashion, or photography. Make a list of things you love, things you are passionate about, and areas where you naturally excel. Then, make a second list of things that drain your energy, skills you don't enjoy using, or jobs you would do anything to avoid. These two lists are powerful because they offer clarity. Sometimes, people feel lost in finding their purpose, but the answers often lie in what we already know about ourselves.

However, passion alone isn't always enough. Some of the most successful people didn't start off being the best at what they do, they developed their skills over time. If you love something but don't yet feel confident in it, that doesn't mean it's not part of your purpose. It simply means growth is required. Skill and passion go hand in hand; refining your strengths will lead to greater fulfillment and success in the long run. Don't let perfectionism hold you back, embrace the learning process.

Once you've reflected on your strengths and weaknesses, consider what comes next. How can you take steps toward aligning with what you love? Maybe it's researching careers that match your strengths, taking a class, or talking to someone who has experience in a field that excites you. Your purpose doesn't have to be a grand revelation, it often unfolds step by step. What's important is that you start paying attention to the things that make you come alive and take small, intentional actions in that direction.

Consider making your two lists right now, one of your strengths and passions and another of things you know you'd rather avoid. After making these lists, reflect on any patterns or realizations that emerge. What stands out to you? Are there steps you can take to move closer to your true calling? Your destiny is already within you, it's waiting for you to discover and embrace it.

Affirmation: I trust that my passions and talents are guiding me toward my true calling, and I am open to the path unfolding before me.

Journal Prompt: Reflect on your natural strengths and passions. How do they align with your current path? Are there areas where you feel out of alignment with your true purpose? What steps can you take to move closer to work that feels fulfilling and authentic to who you are?

Mistakes

You're probably going to make a few mistakes along the way. Yup! I'm sorry. Maybe that's not something you want or need to hear, but it shouldn't come as a surprise either. We all make mistakes and will continue to do so as imperfect, fallible beings. What may be a surprise is that it's okay to make mistakes. It's okay to forgive yourself, put it behind you, and move forward. We're all imperfect beings, so when you make a mistake, give yourself grace, forgive yourself, learn from it, and then move on. Treasure the lessons and leave the rest behind.

Not all mistakes are the same, though. Some are minor, those everyday missteps that are easy to brush off and correct with little effort. These types of mistakes don't carry a heavy burden and often feel like mere speed bumps. For these, it's enough to acknowledge, adjust, and keep moving forward.

There are other mistakes that feel much heavier. These are the ones that require more thought and reflection, mistakes that might involve others or affect your goals more deeply. For these, it's important to take the time to honestly evaluate the situation.

If others are involved, be sincere in your apology, make amends, and own your part. But even in these situations, remember the importance of forgiving yourself and moving forward. It may take more time to release the weight of a heavier mistake, but daily grace is your ally. Remember, it's all part of the process of growth.

Many of us tend to be hard on ourselves after making a mistake, worrying that people are judging us, or that our mistakes will follow us, forever defining our character. Sometimes, we just plain give up because we dwell on the mistake and not the lesson; we allow mistakes to keep us from moving forward because we're afraid to repeat them.

This is where a growth mindset becomes invaluable. Instead of viewing mistakes as failures, shift your perspective to see them as opportunities for growth. When you make a mistake, it's not a sign that you're incapable; it's a sign that you're learning, evolving, and trying. Embrace the idea that mistakes are stepping stones rather than roadblocks.

Don't waste your energy worrying about those who you think are judging you— they might be, or they might not be. Either way, it doesn't change the fact that everyone of us are out there making mistakes, learning, and growing. No one has it all figured out, and no one is immune to failure. What truly matters isn't whether others are watching or criticizing, it's how you respond to your own missteps. Every mistake is an opportunity to learn, to evolve, and to become a stronger, wiser version of yourself. Instead of dwelling on what others might think, focus on what you can take away from the experience and use it to propel yourself forward.

Affirmation: I release the weight of my past mistakes and embrace them as steppingstones to growth. I forgive myself with compassion, knowing that I am always learning, evolving, and worthy of grace.

Journal Prompt: Think about a recent mistake you've made. Was it a minor misstep or a heavier mistake that required deeper reflection? How did you respond to it? Looking back, what lesson can you take from it, and how can you apply a growth mindset to move forward with grace?

Change Is Not Optional

Change is one thing you can always count on. It's not optional. We will always be guaranteed change occurring in the world, in our circumstances, and within ourselves as we grow. Sometimes, change is predictable, and other times, it's completely unexpected. But one thing remains true, we must embrace the fact that change is inevitable.

If you're someone who doesn't really care for change, I encourage you to learn to embrace it. No, it's not always easy. Even positive changes can present challenges. It forces us to step outside our comfort zone, leave behind the familiar, disrupt our routine, and present us with new obstacles. But we are transformed through change, it promotes healthy inner growth, encouraging us to revamp our perspective with the thrill of new experiences.

Perhaps you are someone who embraces change. If so, you're in good company, as I personally love and crave change. I rearrange my furniture often, try new restaurants and order different food, listen to a wide array of music, take on new challenges and it's why I moved to the beach—because I view change as an adventure! I get to see something new, try something different, meet new people, do something I've never done before, learn about the world around me and discover more about myself in the process. If I don't like whatever is changing in my life, I know that's okay too, because nothing is permanent, I can always adjust, move on to something else, or simply wait it out. Because of change, we're never stuck indefinitely, we have options, and our circumstances are not locked in.

The Unexpected Gifts of Change

It's natural to fear the unknown, but think about this, what if the changes you resist today are leading you toward something better? Some of the most significant blessings in life come disguised as unexpected change. A job loss might lead to a dream career. A failed relationship could make space for deeper self-discovery and a healthier connection down the road. Even struggles can shape us into stronger, wiser, and more resilient people.

Instead of fearing change, try asking yourself:

- *What new opportunities could this bring?*

- *How could this be happening for me, not to me?*

- *What am I learning about myself in this process?*

Shifting Your Mindset on Change

If embracing change feels challenging, consider shifting your perspective with a growth mindset. See yourself as capable and open to new experiences rather than resisting them. Instead of thinking, *"I don't know if I can handle this,"* try telling yourself, *"This is an opportunity for growth."* By reframing uncertainty as an opportunity, you can begin to see the unknown not as something to fear but as a doorway to new possibilities. Trust that discomfort is a natural part of growth, every transformation requires stepping beyond what feels familiar, and it's in that stretch where real growth happens. While you may not always have control over the change itself, you do have control over your attitude, your response, and your ability to adapt. Shifting your mindset in this way allows you to embrace change with confidence rather than resistance.

Building Adaptability

Change doesn't always have to be massive or life-altering. Training yourself to be adaptable in small ways can help build resilience for when bigger changes arise. Simple shifts in your daily life can strengthen your ability to embrace the unknown with confidence. Try taking a different route to work or home to break out of routine or switch up your daily habits to welcome variety. Experiment with new activities, restaurants, or hobbies to cultivate a sense of curiosity and adventure. Challenge yourself to say "yes" to something that slightly scares you, pushing past comfort zones and proving your own capability. Practicing mindfulness can also help you stay present, allowing you to focus on the moment rather than worrying about what lies ahead. These small steps create a foundation of adaptability, making it easier to navigate life's inevitable changes with ease and confidence.

Change is not the enemy; it is a teacher, a guide, and a doorway to new opportunities. Even when it's difficult, trust that you are capable of navigating it. When you embrace change, you embrace growth, resilience, and possibility.

Affirmation: Change is a doorway to growth. I trust in my ability to adapt and thrive.

Journal Prompt: Think about a time when you experienced a significant change in your life. How did you feel about it at the time, and how do you feel about it now? What did that change teach you about yourself, your resilience, or your ability to adapt? If you're currently facing a change, how can you shift your mindset to see it as an opportunity for growth?

Let's Not Compare

I've often heard people say, *"I'm not going to complain about my problems because other people have it much worse."* Perhaps you've said this phrase yourself at one time or another or at least thought the same thing. It is true that not everyone has the same challenges to overcome, and some experience very difficult things. However, what one person is going through does not diminish what you are going through, the struggles you face, the feelings attached to that struggle, or the impact on your life, health, and well-being.

If you often compare your struggles to someone else's, it's time to refocus. We shouldn't compare ourselves to anyone else and should instead have empathy and compassion for both them and ourselves. If we see, hear of, or know someone struggling through a difficult time, offer them help and be supportive without comparing our troubles to theirs or their troubles to someone else's.

Social media plays a significant role in fostering comparison, often amplifying the belief that others are living better, more exciting lives. With curated posts showcasing only the highlights of people's experiences, it's easy to forget that these platforms rarely tell the whole story. This selective portrayal of life can create an unrealistic standard that leads to feelings of inadequacy, making us feel like our struggles are less valid or not worthy of attention. When we compare our behind-the-scenes to someone else's highlight reel, it's important to remember that everyone faces challenges, even if they're not visible online. Being mindful of the content we consume and taking breaks from social media can help us reconnect with our own experiences, without getting lost in a false narrative of perfection.

Constantly comparing ourselves to others can have a detrimental effect on our mental health. It can lead to feelings of inadequacy, low self-esteem, and a sense of unworthiness, as we often focus on what we perceive to be other people's successes, forgetting that everyone faces their own struggles. This cycle of comparison can cause anxiety, depression, and a sense of hopelessness, as we feel that we are falling short or not measuring up. Rather than helping us grow, comparison can keep us stuck in negative thought patterns that hinder our ability to embrace our unique journey. The key to breaking this cycle is to remind ourselves that our worth is not defined by others and that our struggles, no matter how small they may seem in comparison, are valid and important.

Minimizing or avoiding our feelings and emotions because we are comparing ourselves to others will hinder us from pursuing the self-care and healing we need to move forward. Instead of falling into the trap of comparison, try shifting your perspective with a few simple steps. First, practice gratitude without guilt, acknowledge both your blessings and your struggles, because gratitude and personal challenges can coexist. Next, reframe your thoughts. Instead of thinking, *"I shouldn't feel this way because others have it worse,"* try reminding yourself, *"My feelings are valid, and I deserve support."* Finally, seek connection rather than comparison. When you hear about someone else's struggles, focus on supporting them and learning from shared experiences rather than comparing your situation to theirs. These shifts can help you honor your own journey and foster compassion for both yourself and others.

Vulnerability is often seen as a weakness, but in reality, it is one of the most powerful tools for personal growth and connection. When we allow ourselves to be vulnerable, we open the door to true healing and intimacy with others. Embracing vulnerability means accepting our imperfections, fears, and struggles without the need for validation or comparison. It creates a space for genuine connections, as others can see our authenticity and respond with empathy. By practicing vulnerability, we invite the opportunity to learn, grow, and be supported in ways that wouldn't be possible if we were hiding behind a facade of perfection. Vulnerability allows us to be real with ourselves and others, creating an environment where healing and growth can truly take place.

Each situation we face has the potential to strengthen our character and be used for growth. Instead of measuring your pain against someone else's, choose self-compassion. Your struggles matter. Your feelings are valid.

Affirmation: I honor my feelings and my journey. I release comparison and embrace my own path to healing and growth.

Journal Prompt: Think about a time when you compared your struggles to someone else's. How did that comparison affect your ability to process your emotions and seek support? What might have happened if you had given yourself permission to feel and heal without comparison? Moving forward, how can you show more compassion to yourself in your own struggles?

Unlearning What Life Is Supposed To Look Like

Do you have a specific idea of what you feel life is "supposed to look like" or how it's supposed to unfold? If so, where did that idea come from? Take some time to really think about who or what it was that molded your perspective of idealistic adulthood—whether it was your parents, other family members, TV, church, or the lack of one or more of these in your life. None of these is inherently bad or good, but it's essential to recognize that times have changed, people have changed, and our world has changed. The societal expectations placed on us can influence the way we define success, happiness, and fulfillment. These expectations often become internalized, shaping how we measure our worth and directing the choices we make. The pressure to live up to an idealized image can have a lasting effect on our identity and self-esteem.

I stayed in a toxic marriage for years because that's what was expected. I grew up saying I'd never get divorced, because the values instilled in me opposed the concept of divorce; my husband knew that and used it to his advantage. This was not an isolated experience but one that reflects the larger narrative of how deeply we can be affected by societal and familial norms. It wasn't until I started to reevaluate my life and release myself from the notion that my choices had to align with the expectations of others that I began to find true freedom.

By no means am I encouraging anyone to make a life-altering decision, or question any decision that is based on your values. I am encouraging constant reevaluation. When we take the time to critically assess what's driving our decisions, we empower ourselves to think freely and independently. Life does not come with a one-size-fits-all mold; it's meant to look different for everyone. Embracing this diversity is an important step in reclaiming your life on your own terms. We live in a world where nontraditional paths and diverse journeys are more common than ever before. When we stop comparing ourselves to others, we create space for the freedom to build a life that reflects our unique experiences, desires, and values.

Sometimes, the most difficult part of this journey is letting go of the fear of judgment. It can be hard to navigate the uncertainty that comes with making decisions that deviate from what we've been taught or what others expect of us. We fear being seen as "failure" or "irresponsible" for not fitting into society's neatly packaged idea of success. But, by reframing our thoughts, we can start to see that we are worthy of support and empathy, just like anyone else. Letting go of the pressure to meet others' standards means giving ourselves permission to feel our emotions without guilt or shame. Embracing vulnerability is one way to begin this journey of self-empowerment.

As you reevaluate your life's direction, it's important to consider how far you've come from the expectations that once guided your decisions. Ask yourself: What did I learn from this experience? Have I been living based on what others expect of me, or have I been true to myself? Often, we make life choices that feel comfortable or familiar because they align with the ideals we were taught, but those same choices can sometimes hold us back from achieving our fullest potential. It's essential to take a step back from time to time and ask whether our decisions are aligned with our true values or simply out of habit.

In this process, one of the most powerful tools is self-compassion. You don't have to have it all figured out; it's okay to not have a defined path. It's normal to feel grief, fear, excitement, and relief as you let go of old ideals and embrace new possibilities. Giving yourself permission to feel those emotions without judgment can be incredibly freeing. Remember, the journey toward living authentically isn't linear—it's a process that unfolds in its own time.

The path that is right for you may look completely different from what others around you are doing, and that's perfectly okay. Surrounding

In a world where diversity is the one constant, we should celebrate that we all have our own ways of navigating life. The pressure to fit into a cookie-cutter mold no longer exists, and the people who are thriving are often those who choose unconventional paths. Embrace your individuality and the uniqueness of your own journey, knowing that it's not just okay, but essential, to create a life that's authentic to you. Let go of the constraints of societal expectations and embrace the opportunity to shape a life that truly reflects who you are and what you value. You have the power to create something beautiful, and it doesn't need to look like anyone else's version of success.

Affirmation: I release the pressure to live up to societal expectations. I trust in my unique path, and I embrace the freedom to create a life that reflects my true self. I am worthy of living authentically and pursuing what brings me joy and fulfillment.

Journal Prompt: Take a moment to reflect on any expectations, whether from family, society, or your own past, that may have influenced your life choices. What areas of your life have you been living out of alignment with your true desires? How can you start to shift toward a life that feels more authentic to you? Write about one small step you can take today to move toward embracing your unique journey.

Self Determination

Before the discovery of my second husband's affair, I began the year excited to watch his swearing-in ceremony as he was recently elected mayor of our small town. This was a goal we'd spent the entire previous year campaigning for. He'd worked hard to reach this moment in his life, and I fully supported him every step of the way. Finally, his shining moment was before us, and I was happy to be "the woman behind the man," his ambitious supporter who had helped him achieve this extraordinary goal of his. I was proud to be his biggest supporter, his avid helper, and his champion.

Little did I know that by the end of the very same year, I'd close out my year sitting on a wooden bench in a sleepy little beach town, alone, listening to the sound of the waves crashing in front of me, with the music of "The Cascades" playing in the background. It was late December, and the beach was all but empty, just a few locals taking an afternoon walk and someone in the background cleaning out their car while Rhythm of the Rain soothed my soul and filled me with peace. How quickly, how unexpectedly, and how drastically things can change sometimes. Sitting beside the ocean, taking in my surroundings and the peacefulness of it all, I reflected on the previous year. I knew everything that happened, every bad thing, every tear, every heartache, all the confusion, and all the decisions I had to make, led me to this moment where I felt absolute peace. I knew I was exactly where I was meant to be. Whatever lay before me was also undoubtedly meant for me, and I was no longer afraid.

There were some decisions I had no say in, things thrown my way I'd rather not have faced, and many challenges to overcome. I was knocked down harder than ever, but after taking it day by day for a while, I picked up the pieces and put myself back together. I had many decisions to make, most importantly, refusing to allow my situation to determine my outcome. I was determined to turn the negative into a positive, so I changed my thinking from believing something was taken away from me to believing I was given an opportunity. I was down bigtime. I was down for a while, but I chose not to stay there. It wasn't where I belong, and it's not where you belong either. You have the power to put the pieces together and refuse to allow any person or situation to rob you of the blessed life you desire and deserve. Gradually, you'll turn any negatives into positives.

It wasn't an easy journey, and it took time, but I slowly learned how to find peace amidst the uncertainty. For a long time, I felt like everything was falling apart. But the more I surrendered to the uncertainty of it all, the more I realized that peace could exist even in the unknown. I didn't have to have all the answers right away, and I didn't need to control every aspect of my life. Sometimes, we have to let go of the need to control everything and trust that life will unfold as it should. In the quiet moments, especially during those days when I wasn't sure what came next, I found that peace came when I stopped resisting change and began to accept it as a natural part of life. It didn't mean that I had to enjoy the discomfort, but I learned to stop fighting against it. That made all the difference.

As I began to rebuild, I had to reconnect with myself. For so long, my identity had been intertwined with my relationship, my role as a wife, and supporting someone else's dreams. In the aftermath of the betrayal, I had to rediscover who I was outside of those roles. What did I want for myself? Who was I without the expectations of others? I had to allow myself the space to explore new passions, to set new goals, and to remember the woman I had been before I became so enmeshed in another person's life. That process wasn't immediate, but as I embraced my own individuality, I grew stronger. I began to realize that I could be whole on my own, and that was a transformative realization.

Finally, as I turned my pain into power, I began to focus on actionable ways to shift my mindset from negative to positive. One of the first steps I took was shifting my perspective. I stopped seeing my struggles as something being taken from me and instead started to view them as opportunities for growth. I knew I couldn't change what had happened, but I could change how I responded to it. I started to focus on gratitude, not just for the blessings in my life but also for the lessons hidden in the hardship. There were countless lessons that came from this experience, lessons about resilience, self-worth, and the importance of creating boundaries.

I also gave myself the freedom to let go of old patterns. Instead of clinging to the idea that I had to have everything figured out immediately, I embraced the idea of taking small steps forward each day. Some days were harder than others, but those small steps added up. I started journaling more frequently, focusing on what I could control—my thoughts, my responses, and my actions. I spent more time with myself, learning to listen to my inner voice and trust my instincts. As I focused on these things, I began to see the negatives transform. I wasn't just surviving; I was evolving into a version of myself that was even stronger, more aligned with my authentic desires.

Affirmation: I am resilient, and every challenge I face is an opportunity for growth. I trust myself to navigate uncertainty and create a life aligned with my true purpose. I am worthy of peace, happiness, and all the good things that are coming my way.

Journal Prompt: Reflecting on the changes and challenges you've faced, how have you transformed as a person? What strengths have you discovered within yourself that you didn't know existed before? Write about a time when a difficult situation led to personal growth. What lessons did you learn, and how can you carry those lessons forward into the future?

Embrace Yourself, Your Journey and What You Believe

Your destiny is who you are and has been inside you from the beginning, all that's left is for you to take the first step. Taking that scary, uncomfortable, unfamiliar step toward an unknown future can feel daunting. It's natural to experience self-doubt when venturing into the unknown. If you find yourself questioning whether you're capable, remind yourself that it's a part of the process. Self-doubt is not a signal to stop, but an invitation to grow. To build confidence, embrace the discomfort of uncertainty, knowing that it's through these moments of doubt that you will discover the strength, wisdom, and resilience you didn't know you had.

As you embark on this crusade of self-discovery, pursuing passions ablaze with possibility, believe in yourself and your ability to achieve what you set out to do. There will be setbacks along the way. Sometimes, things won't go as planned, and you'll face closed doors. But understand that these moments are not failures; they're necessary parts of the process. Every setback holds a lesson, and every failure is an opportunity to learn, grow, and realign with your purpose. Those closed doors are not meant to keep you out; they're guiding you toward a better path. It's through trials, tribulations, and reflections that you gain the insight necessary to move forward with even greater clarity. Remember, success is not defined by avoiding failure, but by your ability to rise from it.

As you walk your path, be sure to listen to your inner voice. Trust your intuition and align with your core values as you navigate challenges. It's easy to get distracted by external expectations or others' opinions, but true fulfillment comes from honoring your authentic self and aligning your actions with what truly matters to you. Stay grounded in your values, and trust that the right decisions will flow from this alignment. Allow your intuition to be a guiding force when faced with choices, whether big or small. Your journey is uniquely yours, and it's essential to honor that truth.

It's easy to expect everything to unfold in a linear way, but the journey toward your destiny is rarely straight and narrow. It takes time, and sometimes it requires more patience than we'd like to admit. The road to your purpose isn't always clear, and the timing may not always make sense. But persist, even when it feels like you're not getting anywhere. Trust that every small step, every moment of discomfort, and every challenge is leading you exactly where you need to be. And know that persistence is key, the more you keep going, the closer you get to your true potential.

Throughout all of this, remember to practice gratitude. Gratitude helps us recognize the beauty and growth that come with the process, especially in moments of struggle. Reflect on how far you've come, even if the progress feels slow. Appreciate each milestone, no matter how small, because those moments of progress are a reflection of your commitment and determination. Gratitude fosters the mindset needed to see the bigger picture and reminds you that you're right where you need to be. It also reinforces that no matter the external circumstances, you are always growing and becoming.

Your unique path in life is what makes it extraordinary.

Affirmation: I trust the journey of my life and embrace each step, knowing that every challenge and every triumph is guiding me toward my true purpose. I am exactly where I need to be.

Journal Prompt: Where do you see your future self? What small steps can you take today to align more closely with your true purpose?

References

1. Geoffrey James, "According To Neuroscience Confidence Is Contageous, But Not For The Reasons You Think | Inc.com," Inc, November 8 2019, https://www.inc.com/geoffrey-james/if-youve-got-this-1-character-trait youll-probably-be-successful-according-to-neuroscience.html

Robyn is available for coaching or speaking engagements for small or large groups and workshops.

Visit robynmichelle.life for details

ABOUT THE AUTHOR

Robyn Michelle is an INFJ Virgo, proud Gen X beach-loving, tree-hugging, sunglasses collecting, cheese-addicted eternal optimist. She believes in the power of positive thinking, that everyone has a unique purpose and heart of resilience, and we can all achieve the things that set our hearts on fire. Robyn does her best writing in local coffee shops by the beach. When she's not jotting away every little thought that comes to mind you can find her on or near the water listening to groovy music and sipping hot coffee.

Check out Robyn's socials
www.robynmichelle.life
Robyn Michelle on Facebook
@robnmichelle007 on Instagram and Ticktok